FINANCIAL SECRETS OF MY WEALTHY GRANDPARENTS

FINANCIAL SECRETS OF MY WEALTHY GRANDPARENTS

A Guide To Help Retirees Avoid Financial Mistakes and
Create an Inspiring Financial Future

Matthew Tuttle

CFP®, MBA, President of Tuttle Wealth Management, LLC

iUniverse, Inc.
New York Lincoln Shanghai

Financial Secrets of My Wealthy Grandparents
A Guide To Help Retirees Avoid Financial Mistakes and Create an
Inspiring Financial Future

Copyright © 2006 by Matthew Tuttle

iUniverse books may be ordered through booksellers or by contacting:

iUniverse
2021 Pine Lake Road, Suite 100
Lincoln, NE 68512
www.iuniverse.com
1-800-Authors (1-800-288-4677)

ISBN-13: 978-0-595-40631-9 (pbk)
ISBN-13: 978-0-595-84996-3 (ebk)
ISBN-10: 0-595-40631-9 (pbk)
ISBN-10: 0-595-84996-2 (ebk)

Printed in the United States of America

CONTENTS

ACKNOWLEDGEMENTS

Throughout my career as a financial planner I have been influenced by a number of people and companies who have also influenced the contents of this book. Special thanks to:

- Bill Bachrach from Bachrach & Associates for his work with Values-Based Financial Planning™. Specifically his training on the importance of values and delegating your finances to an advisor you can trust.
- Larry Klein from NF Communications. Specifically for his expertise on the financial concerns of seniors—-long term care, IRAs, investments, and estate planning.
- SEI Investments for their groundbreaking work with Goals Based Investing.
- Fidelity Investments for their studies on longevity and safe withdrawal rates.

INTRODUCTION

Like most people, I had two sets of grandparents. I had wealthy grandparents and poor grandparents. Both were the second generation of their families in this country, and both lived the American dream. Both of my grandfathers started and ran their own successful businesses, which they sold when they retired. They both retired at about the same age with about the same amount of money. Both couples had the same dreams: retire someplace warm, play golf, travel, and spend time with their children and grandchildren. My wealthy grandparents, however, left a $2 million estate, while my poor grandparents ended up broke.

Both sets of grandparents had an impact on my decision to be a financial planner. When I was young, they used to give me shares of stock instead of money or toys. They helped me track the share prices and talked to me about finance. I had insight into their financial decisions. Later on, it became obvious to me what my wealthy grandparents had done to become wealthy and what my poor grandparents had done to become poor.

Today's retirees face issues that their parents and grandparents never had to deal with. Medical science has increased life expectancy, but that causes a number of problems for retirees: the need for long-term care, inflation, and the need to generate income for thirty years or more, just to name a few.

My Wealthy Grandparents

My wealthy grandparents realized that if they lived a long life, they would need to invest in stocks, and they didn't let their emotions dictate their investment decisions. They knew how to set up their portfolio to deliver a lifetime income, while considering inflation. My wealthy grandparents also hired an advisor whom they trusted to manage their affairs.

My Poor Grandparents

My poor grandparents didn't plan on living long after retirement, but they did. They set their investment portfolio to generate income, but they didn't plan for inflation. They saw their friends and neighbors getting sick and needing long-term care, but they didn't think it would happen to them. My poor grandparents always handled their money themselves.

What You Will Learn

There are a number of books that tell young people how to plan for retirement, but there are very few that tell them what to do once they get there. This book will teach you why my wealthy grandparents stayed wealthy and why my poor grandparents ran out of money. In this book you will learn the following:

- A new way to look at managing your portfolio, called Goals-Based Investing
- The right way to take income from your portfolio so that you don't outlive your money
- What to look for in a long-term care insurance policy
- The biggest mistake most investors make
- The biggest mistakes people make with their IRAs
- How to design a financial strategy that inspires you
- And much more!

This book contains a wealth of information that will ensure a bright financial future. For you to get the most value from it, however, you need to be aware of the one phenomenon that causes many retirees to procrastinate about improving their financial lives—the fear of the mistake.

Fear of the Mistake

Financial mistakes are magnified in retirement. If a thirty-five-year-old makes a mistake, there is still time to recover. If a sixty-five-year-old makes the same mistake, it can be devastating. Retirees understand this very well. In my years of financial planning for retirees, I have noticed that many fear making a financial mistake more than anything else.

When my poor grandparents realized that their financial plan wasn't working, they didn't change it. They had always managed their finances by themselves, and they continued to do that. They knew that they were making mistakes, but they kept asking themselves, "What if we make changes and our situation becomes even worse?" They knew what they were doing with their money was wrong, but it gave them a certain comfort. Making changes may or may not have made things better, but that uncertainty frightened them. For my poor grandparents inaction was the mistake.

You should not change your financial strategy with the wind. You should be careful when making financial decisions. Yet sometimes this attitude can be counterproductive. If you know that your current financial plan isn't working, you need to make changes.

The book will show you how through the following sections:

Section I: Your Financial Foundation. Section I talks about where you want to go financially and where you are now. Some people might be tempted to skip to the "good stuff," to learn about investment strategies, estate-planning strategies, and so forth. Most people have no real strategy, no real sense whether they are making smart choices. The key to making smart choices about your money is to get clear on what you want and why. Once you have defined the financial future you want, the next step is to get clear on your present financial reality. By defining your future and your present, you can see the gap between where you are now and where you want to be.

Section II: Strategies for Financial Success. Section II will cover the main areas of your financial life: investments, IRAs, long-term care, estate planning, income, and so forth. Here we will talk about key issues and strategies you must be aware of.

Section III: Putting It All Together. Section III will help you figure out what type of investor you are: a do–it–yourselfer, a collaborator, or a delegator. It will also give you some tips to find a trusted advisor who can put your financial plan in place so that you can spend your time doing the things you really enjoy.

Let's get started.

SECTION I

YOUR FINANCIAL FOUNDATION

CHAPTER 1

PUT YOUR MONEY WHERE
YOUR VALUES ARE

Sandra came into my office with a problem. She and her husband, Scott, had amassed a portfolio worth millions of dollars, but something wasn't quite right. When I asked Sandra what was important to her she said, "Having a sense of security." Scott had always managed the finances and had told her everything would be fine, but she wasn't sure. I took one look at how much they had and what their goals were. I assured her that she had enough money to achieve all of her goals and then some. Her mood immediately changed and she smiled; she finally felt a sense of security.

It may seem strange to start a book about financial planning by talking about your values. You may wonder, "What do values have to do with financial planning?"

We all have goals. Your goal might be something as simple as wanting more money, or it could be as grandiose as wanting to retire early and sail around the world in your yacht. Why do you want those things? If you want more money, do you really want more pieces of green paper with pictures of dead famous people on them? No, you want the feelings that having more money will give you, feelings like security, independence, freedom, and power. Those feelings are your values. Your goals are what you want in your life. Your values are why you want them. Values are the emotional payoff for achieving your goals. It doesn't make sense to try to figure out how (your financial strategy) and what (your goals) until you know why (your values).

Most financial planning is based on achieving your goals, but that is not enough. Simply achieving your goals alone will not fulfill you. Not fulfilling your values leads to frustration and disappointment.

Since your values are important to you, it is crucial that your financial decisions be in line with your values. These decisions will eventually become your reality. Let's say that having a sense of security was

3

important to you. You might accumulate millions of dollars, but if you didn't feel secure you would still not be happy.

As a financial advisor I concentrate on values surrounding money, an area in which people do things in conflict with their values all the time. Consider the busy executive who works a hundred hours a week and whose primary value is to spend time with his family. He may be achieving financial success, but it is unlikely he will ever be truly happy because his life is in conflict with his values.

Money is not the most important thing in your life, but your financial health directly impacts every other aspect of your life. When your finances are in line, your relationships are better, your mental health is better, your physical health is better, and your spiritual health is better. The path to financial health begins by determining your values and making sure your financial affairs are in line with them. For example, you might value providing for your family, but, if something happens to you, you may not have a will or life insurance. Or you may value safety and security, but your portfolio is full of Internet stocks.

My grandparents all valued security and independence very highly. My wealthy grandparents had a plan in place that gave them a feeling of security and independence during their entire retirement. My poor grandparents had no plan in place. They ended up with no security being dependent on others for their care.

I have a friend who is thirty-seven years old. For a number of years he worked on Wall Street and earned a six-figure salary with seven-figure bonuses. He is one of the happiest people I know. Not because he makes so much money—he lives in a modest house, drives used cars, doesn't have the nicest clothes, and tries to save as much money as possible. He is happy because he values giving something back to society. He saves his money religiously so that now he can retire and spend his time doing volunteer work. Ultimately, his money and the choices he makes concerning his money have made his values a reality. He could have enjoyed a much more luxurious lifestyle, but that would have been in conflict with his values. Other people look at what he does and can't understand it because they have different values.

On the other hand, I have people who come into my office every day who are not happy with their finances. They value things like security and safety, but their financial decisions make them feel insecure and unsafe. They spend more than they earn and put any savings into volatile investments. Their financial plan is in conflict with their values.

I am going to tell you something you have probably never heard before, but believe me this is true—sometimes couples fight about money (I know you don't, I am talking about other couples). This book will not teach you how to fix this—there are other books on that topic—but I think one of the main reasons this happens is that couples often have different values when it comes to money. One spouse may value safety and security while another spouse may value freedom and excitement. Do you think the decisions they make about their money will be a little different? I think so.

Too often people have no idea what is important to them. If you have ever had trouble making a financial decision, perhaps you were not clear on your values. Once you know your values, your decisions become easy.

The first step in aligning your money with your values is to get clear on your values. Here is a process you can use to clarify your values:

Step 1: To find out your values, you simply need to ask, "What's important to me?" Since this book is concerned with your values regarding money, the question should be, "What's important about money to me?" Record your answers below. There is no wrong or silly answer, just record what comes to mind.

When you are doing this exercise, you may come up with answers like "I want to have more money" or "retirement." These are goals, and we will talk more about those in the next chapter. We want goals for the feelings they will give us; they are a means to an end. To get your values, you need to figure out why you want to achieve that goal. Ask yourself, "What's important about (my goal) to me?" So, for example, you may want more money because it gives you a sense of security. In this case, security is the value that you want to record.

Step 2: Take the answer to the first question and ask, "What's important about having (first answer) to me?" So, for example, if your first answer was a sense of security, the next question is, "What's important about having a sense of security to me?"

Step 3: Take your answers to the first two questions and ask, "If I had (first answer) and (second answer), what would that ultimately do for me?" So, for example, if you answered security to the first question and peace of mind to the second question, the third question would be, "If I had a sense of security and peace of mind, what would that ultimately do for me?"

Here Are Some Examples of Values:

Freedom

Security

Passion

Success

Love

Security

Adventure

Power

Comfort

Independence

Contributing

Happiness

Achieving

Peace of mind

Making a difference

Write down your answers to the values questions.

1. What's important about money to me? _____

2. What's important about (first answer) to me? _____

3. If I had (first answer) and (second answer), what would that ultimately do for me?

_____

_____

Then have your spouse or partner do the same.

1. What's important about money to me? _____

2. What's important about (first answer) to me? _____

3. If I had (first answer) and (second answer), what would that ultimately do for me?

_____

_____

Please make sure you do answer these questions with your spouse or partner. Since you will be planning your financial future together, it will be enlightening for you both to be clear on each other's values regarding money.

Take a look at your list. Having a financial strategy, which this book will give you, will help you fulfill your values. If that doesn't seem exciting to you, then you didn't really commit to doing the exercise. Truly identify your values. Go back to work until you have some compelling answers. This is the list that will inspire you to take action and will guide you toward making smart choices about your money.

CHAPTER 2

WHERE DO YOU WANT TO GO?

You have decided to take a trip, but you are not quite sure where; you just know that you want to go someplace. With no real destination in mind, you get into the car, start the ignition, and pull out of the driveway. Which way do you go? Of course you would never start out on a trip without a destination in mind, but this is how most people approach their financial planning. In my classes and seminars, I am often asked my opinion on different financial products. My answer is always the same: it's impossible to give advice on what financial product to buy without knowing where you want to go first. Just like in the previous chapter, you need to know what you want before you can figure out how you are going to get it.

The Wall Street marketing machine has done a great job of convincing people that all they need for a secure financial future is the next hot thing. Most people have portfolios full of financial products purchased through the years with no real rhyme or reason. No matter how old you are, you still have a future, and it will be here whether you plan for it or not. You can either let your financial future happen by chance, or you can design the future you want ahead of time. It's up to you.

In my speeches I always ask the audience how many people have written goals. Out of thirty people, one or two people usually raise their hands. Most people are missing out on the power of setting goals.

I heard about a study that was done years ago with a graduating class at an Ivy League university. The class was asked if they had a written set of goals and a plan for their achievement. Not surprisingly, only 3 percent of the class had written goals. Years later, the researchers interviewed the surviving members of the class. They found that the 3 percent with written goals had happier and more fulfilling lives. While happiness is subjective, what is not subjective is that the 3 percent with written goals had amassed a net worth in excess of the other 97 percent combined!

Most people are familiar with comedic actor Jim Carrey, but very few people know how he got where he is today. I heard a story that at one point Carrey was so poor that he had to live in a van. He decided what he wanted to do, and he wrote himself a $10 million dollar check, which he carried around in his wallet until he could cash it. Only a few years later, he could command over $10 million per movie (*Jim Carrey 1997, Oprah Winfrey Show*). How do these examples relate to you? Study after study has shown the value of written goals, but most people have never taken the time to figure out what they really want out of life.

Our only experience with goal setting usually comes on New Year's. We might be sitting around a table with friends, maybe there is some alcohol involved, and everyone feels pressure to come up with a New Years resolution. We might resolve to lose weight, but then we are usually back on the couch by January 3 eating a big bag of potato chips. Most people fail at setting goals because their goals are not inspiring, specific, and in writing and because they have no real plan for achievement.

We talked in chapter 1 about fulfilling your values. The way to fulfill your values is to set and achieve goals. How do you set goals that work? The goals need to have the following characteristics:

1. **The goal must be in writing, and you should look at it as often as possible.** The saying "out of sight out of mind" definitely applies here. Unless you put your goal in writing and look at it as often as possible, the other events in your life will take precedence. You will soon forget about your goal. One of the main reasons New Year's resolutions usually fail is because you don't write them down. The only time you remember them is next New Year's when you remember that you resolve to achieve it again this year. Once you have written down all of your goals, you need to prioritize them. You may only have enough resources to make some of your goals a reality, so prioritizing them lets you know where to concentrate your efforts.

2. **The goal must be inspiring.** Which goal would inspire you to take action: I want to be able to pay my bills, or I want to buy a sailboat and sail around the world? The answer is obvious, but often times when I ask retirees what they want the answer is to pay my bills or to have a roof over my head. Your goals *must* be inspiring enough to motivate you to take the actions necessary to achieve them. Don't get me wrong, I am not saying that your goal has to be mas-

sive; it just needs to be inspiring to you. Some people are inspired by the idea of living off of $40,000 per year in retirement, while other people are inspired by the idea of $500,000 per year.

You should never feel that you need to apologize for your goals. Sometimes I will see clients who are embarrassed by their modest or grandiose goals. Your goals are your goals because they are important to you; you shouldn't have to justify them to anyone.

3. **The goal must be specific and measurable.** I want to retire at age sixty-five is not good enough. For a goal to be effective, it must be specific and measurable. When we go through this exercise with clients, we ask them for a specific day they want to achieve their goal by and a specific dollar amount. For example, I want to retire on April 15, 2015, and I want to have $100,000 per year (indexed for inflation) in annual income. Don't be afraid to aim high here. You may have no idea how you are going to achieve your goals, that's OK. Later sections in the book will help clear that up.

My wealthy grandparents had specific goals that they wrote down and reviewed. My poor grandparents did not.

Now that you know what your goals are, imagine the finish line. Imagine that you have achieved your goal. What are two are three words to describe what you are thinking and feeling? Write them down.

Have to Now, Have to Later, Want to Now, or Want to Later

There are four different kinds of financial goals: goals you have to have now, goals you have to have later, goals you want to have now, and goals you want to have later. Have-to-now or have-to-later goals might include things like maintaining your lifestyle, future retirement, paying for college for kids and grandkids, and so forth. Want-to-now and want-to-later goals might be a vacation home, a boat, and other discretionary goals that would be nice to have but are not mandatory. Obviously, the goals you have to have take priority over the goals you want to have.

Let's put this all together. Place your goals in the appropriate boxes below, when you want to accomplish them, how much money the goal requires (in today's dollars), and what you will be thinking and feeling when you accomplish your goal. Again, don't worry if they seem unrealistic or if you have no idea how you will accomplish them; that will come later. For know, have some fun and write down as many goals as you can imagine.

The following questions might help you clarify your goals:

Have to Now Goals: Key Questions
1. Do either you or your spouse currently have any health issues? Does anyone in your family have health issues?
2. With respect to your goals, what do you know that you have to do (i.e., must pay for children's education)?
3. Which things in life do you think are most important right now?
4. Whom do you feel responsible for?
5. Are you expecting any life changes in the next three to five years?
6. With respect to your goals, what do you know that you need to be doing right now?

Want to Now Goals: Key Questions
1. What types of leisure activities are you currently involved in?
2. What are you worried about?
3. How involved are you in your community right now?

4. Have you considered a second career?

5. Are you interested in traveling or other hobbies?

6. With respect to your goals, what would you like to be doing right now?

7. If you could afford to, what would you be doing differently?

Have to Later Goals: Key Questions

1. What do you know that you need to achieve in the future?

2. What would you like your life to look like in five years? Ten years?

3. How do you see your lifestyle changing beyond ten years?

4. Will you need to support anyone else in your family?

5. What is your greatest hope for your family?

6. What is your greatest concern for them?

7. With respect to your goals, what do you know that you need to do in the future?

Want to Later Goals: Key Questions
1. What would you want to do if you had the resources in the future?
2. What are you hoping to leave for your family?
3. What hobbies would you want to be involved in and in what capacity?
4. What philanthropic endeavors would you want to be involved in and in what capacity?
5. Do you possess any particular skills that could benefit your community interests?
6. If you had no heirs, where would you want your wealth to go?
7. Have you considered a second career?
8. Are you interested in traveling or other hobbies?
9. With respect to your goals, what do you know that you want to do in the future?

Source: SEI Investments

Here's an example:

Want to Now Goals Goal: Vacation Home Due Date: 12/31/2006 Dollar Amount: $200,000 down payment What I am thinking and feeling: Yipee!	Want to Later Goals Goal: Buy a Boat Due Date: 12/31/2015 Dollar Amount: $100,000 What I am thinking and feeling: Wow!
Have to Now Goals Goal: College Costs Due Date: 9/1/2006 Dollar Amount: $30,000/year for four years What I am thinking and feeling: Relief!	Have to Later Goals Goal: "The Next Phase" Retirement Due Date: 12/31/2015 Dollar Amount: $10,000/month after-tax income What I am thinking and feeling: Relief, satisfaction, let's pack the suitcases

Now brainstorm with your spouse or partner, and write down all the goals you want to achieve.

Want to Now Goals Goal: Due Date: Dollar Amount: What I am thinking and feeling:	Want to Later Goals Goal: Due Date: Dollar Amount: What I am thinking and feeling:
Goal: Due Date: Dollar Amount: What I am thinking and feeling:	Goal: Due Date: Dollar Amount: What I am thinking and feeling:
Goal: Due Date: Dollar Amount: What I am thinking and feeling:	Goal: Due Date: Dollar Amount: What I am thinking and feeling:

Goal:	Goal:
Due Date:	Due Date:
Dollar Amount:	Dollar Amount:
What I am thinking and feeling:	What I am thinking and feeling:
Have to Now Goals	**Have to Later Goals**
Goal:	Goal:
Due Date:	Due Date:
Dollar Amount:	Dollar Amount:
What I am thinking and feeling:	What I am thinking and feeling:
Goal:	Goal:
Due Date:	Due Date:
Dollar Amount:	Dollar Amount:
What I am thinking and feeling:	What I am thinking and feeling:
Goal:	Goal:
Due Date:	Due Date:
Dollar Amount:	Dollar Amount:
What I am thinking and feeling:	What I am thinking and feeling:
Goal:	Goal:
Due Date:	Due Date:
Dollar Amount:	Dollar Amount:
What I am thinking and feeling:	What I am thinking and feeling:

Now that you know what you want and why you want it, the next step is to get an honest and clear assessment of your current financial reality.

CHAPTER 3

WHERE YOU ARE NOW

Liz came into my office one day. I had asked her to bring all of her financial documents, and she had two big shopping bags full of unopened envelopes and a myriad of papers. She was having all sorts of financial problems and hoped that I could help her. When I asked her simple questions like, "How much debt do you have?" "Where are your assets held?" "How much money do you have in the bank?" and "Do you have a will?" she had no idea.

Imagine that you plan to take a trip to Paris. You know where you want to go and have planned your itinerary in great detail. Excitedly you call the airline to book a ticket to France. The person who answers the phone tells you that he cannot sell you a plane ticket. When you ask why not, they tell you they know where you want to go but not where you are now.

It is impossible to accurately design a financial plan or strategy without a frank assessment of where you are now. Now that you know what's most important to you and you have written goals, it's time to figure out your current financial situation.

The first step is getting organized. A lot of people I meet suffer from what I call the Bag Lady Syndrome. They have bags full of unorganized financial information and can't even answer a simple question like what their net worth is. The more daunting getting organized sounds, the more you need to do it. Get some file folders or notebooks and label them as follows:

1. Tax returns: Put in your most recent return. Keep all returns somewhere you can find them. The IRS can go back as far as they want if they suspect fraud.
2. Retirement accounts: Keep all of your IRAs and 401(k)s.
3. Social Security statements: Keep your most recent Social Security statements in this folder.

4. Investment accounts: Keep all of your non-retirement account statements.
5. Savings & Checking: Keep your bank account statements.
6. Household accounts: Keep information about your home or apartment—leases, improvements, etc..
7. Credit cards: Keep all of your credit card information.
8. Other liabilities: Keep all of your other debts in this folder.
9. Insurance: Keep all your insurance documents.
10. Estate: Keep all of your estate-planning documents.
11. Children's accounts: Keep all statements for children's accounts if applicable.

My wealthy grandparents had very organized finances. They could tell you what their net worth was, how much debt they had, etc. My poor grandparents had no system to organize their finances.

Now that you are organized you need to note four main money areas:
1. Cash reserves and expenses
2. Growth
3. Debt
4. Risk management

1. Cash Reserves and Expenses

This is money you have set aside in case of emergency. This could also be cash set aside in a brokerage account for an emergency (not cash waiting to be invested). This does not include the day-to-day cash in your checking account.

Total cash reserves: $_____

What are your total monthly expenses? $_____
(from the worksheets below)

How many months worth of expenses does this represent? (We generally recommend three to six months.)

(Cash reserves/monthly expenses)

The following worksheets will help you figure your fixed expenses (those that cannot be avoided) and your variable expenses (those that can be avoided). Knowing what you need in your cash reserves and understanding your cash flow will help you plan. If you are not retired yet, this worksheet can also help you get a handle on how much money you may be spending in retirement.

Fixed Monthly Expenses		
	Current	Retirement
Mortgage payment or rent		
Second home mortgage		
Automobile note		
Personal loans		
Credit cards		
Life insurance		
Disability insurance		
Medical insurance		
Long-term care insurance		
Homeowner's insurance		
Automobile insurance		
Umbrella liability insurance		

Federal income taxes		
State income taxes		
FICA		
Real estate taxes		
Other taxes		
Savings (regularly)		
Investments (regularly)		
Retirement plan contributions		
Total Fixed Expenses		

Variable Monthly Expenses		
	Current	**Retirement**
Electricity		
Gas		
Telephone		
Water		
Cable TV		

Home repairs and maintenance		
Home improvements		
Food		
Clothing		
Laundry		
Child care		
Personal care		
Automobile gas and oil		
Automobile repairs, etc.		
Other transportation		
Education expenses		
Entertainment/dining		
Recreation/travel		
Club/association dues		
Hobbies		
Gifts/donations		
Unreimbursed medical and dental expenses		
Miscellaneous		
Total Variable Expenses		

2. Growth

This is the money you have set aside to achieve your goals. Add up your brokerage accounts, mutual funds, IRAs, 401(k)s, 403(b)s, and so on.

How much money have you set aside for growth?

_____

If you are still working, then saving money will probably be a crucial part of your plan. I generally recommend that people save at least 10 percent of their pre-tax income (I often recommend that people save much more than that).

How much are you saving every year (including contributions to your 401(k), IRA, etc.)? _____

What is your pre-tax income? _____

What percentage of your income are you saving?
(Annual savings/Annual pre-tax income)

_____

3. Debt

Debt can be the enemy of growth. For example, it doesn't make sense to have money in a brokerage account earning 7 percent while you owe money on your credit card with 16 percent interest. If you have high-interest debt, then part of your financial strategy should be to pay your debt down and keep it down.

What is your debt?

Amount Owed	To Whom	Interest Rate	Fixed or Variable	Term

4. Risk management

What measures do you have in place if something goes wrong? This is where you would list life insurance, health insurance, disability insurance, long-term care insurance, liability insurance, and your estate-planning documents.

Insurance

Type of Insurance	Who Is Covered	Monthly Premium	Benefit

Estate-Planning Documents

Document	Do You Have It (Yes/No)	Date Drafted
Will		
Living Trust		
Health-Care Proxy		
Durable Power of Attorney		
Living Will		
Marital Trust		
Irrevocable Trust		
Other:		

Now that you have your current financial situation laid out in front of you, what does it tell you? Are you on track to reach your goals or far from it? What areas could use some improvement? The next section will help you focus these strategies.

CHAPTER 4

GETTING STARTED

Now that you know what you want, why you want it, and where you are now, you are ready to begin designing your financial plan.

You now have a compelling vision of what you want for your financial future and a realistic view of your current financial reality. This will serve as a roadmap for all of your financial decisions and the basis for developing the plan that will help you achieve your goals and fulfill your values.

Your Financial Plan

Wouldn't it be great to have a written financial strategy so that no matter what happened in the economy, the world, or the markets, you still felt like you were on track to achieve your goals?

—Bill Bachrach

The next step is to create a financial plan for bridging the gap between where you are now so that you can achieve your goals for the reasons that are important to you. Your goals and your values will serve to inspire you to continue to take action to make the financial future you want a reality.

At a minimum, your plan should include the following:
1. The appropriate amount of cash reserves.
2. A debt reduction/elimination strategy (if applicable)
3. A review or your existing insurances and a review of all types of insurance that exist with an eye toward three things:
   A. Should you own it?
   B. If so, how much should you own?
   C. If so, what kind should you own?
4. An estate plan

5.   An investment plan
6.   An income generation plan

Your written plan should be reviewed a number of times each year to gauge your progress and to see if any changes need to be made due to unforeseen circumstances.

At the end of section I, you should have completed the following:

- Your values are aligned with your goals, and you have clarity about how making smart choices about money affects what's most important to you.
- You have specific financial goals with exact dates and amounts of money needed.
- You are committed to creating a comprehensive written plan, addressing all areas of your financial life.
- You are committed to implement a comprehensive financial plan. Creating a great plan without taking action is like buying an airplane ticket and not taking the trip. Taking action is vital to success.

Section II will cover the main areas of your financial plan, while section III will discuss whether you should do it yourself or get help.

SECTION II

STRATEGIES FOR FINANCIAL SUCCESS

CHAPTER 5

WHAT MY WEALTHY GRANDPARENTS
TAUGHT ME ABOUT INVESTING

Mark came into my office at the height of the bear market. He had run a successful business and had sold it four years earlier for $1 million. He wasn't sure what to do with that much money until he got a call from David. David was a stockbroker from a major Wall Street firm. David told Mark that he needed to be conservative with his investments and recommended a portfolio balanced between stocks and bonds. The advice made sense to Mark, and he agreed to transfer his life savings over to David to manage. A year went by, and Mark got a phone call from David. He suggested a meeting to discuss major changes going on in the market. David explained that the old rules no longer applied and that fortunes could be made in Internet and biotechnology companies. Mark had always had a gambling streak in him, and he trusted David. He decided to move his life savings into Internet and biotech stocks.

At first he was doing well, then very well. He thought David was a genius. Then he noticed his account value was decreasing every month. David told him not to worry; he was advising his other clients that this was a great buying opportunity. By the time Mark came to see me, his original $1 million was worth only $200,000.

Buy low, sell high. Sounds simple doesn't it? Then why do most investors ignore it and do the opposite?

How you invest your money could make the difference between affording a comfortable retirement or outliving your money. Mark learned that the hard way. He had to sell his house and go back to work. There is no way he can ever replace the $800,000 he lost in the market.

My wealthy grandparents had a well thought out investment strategy that they didn't deviate from. My poor grandparents had a portfolio that was not consistent with their lifestyle, values and goals.

In my experience, investors often make one big mistake: chasing after performance.

Chasing after Performance

According to Russ Kinnell, the director of fund research at Morningstar (the largest independent mutual fund rating service), "Had you used the (1999) top 10 performers table as your shopping list, the best you could have done from January 1, 2000 through March, 2003 was to lose a little more than half your money." *Source: Morningstar* Now you may be wondering who would invest that way. Remember back to 1999; the only advice we heard was that Internet and technology stocks were a sure thing.

What about other years? The top performing fund in 1997 was the American Heritage Fund, with a return of 75 percent. If you had invested $10,000 in that fund on January 1, 1998, it would have been worth $955 at the end of 2005 (it was also the top performing fund in 2004). Have I convinced you yet that trying to buy the hot investment isn't the sure road to wealth?

If buying what's hot doesn't work, what does? There are three things that my wealthy grandparents knew about investing that my poor grandparents did not:
1. Avoid large losses.
2. Have a long-term time horizon.
3. Have a methodology that takes your emotions out of the investing equation.

Avoid Large Losses

Below are returns for two mutual funds, the Exciting Fund and the Boring Fund. (I actually made these funds up but you get the point.)

Year	Boring Fund	Exciting Fund
1	7%	10%
2	7%	20%
3	7%	20%
4	7%	-25%
5	7%	10%

The Boring Fund was up 7 percent a year, every year for five years. The Exciting Fund is much more exiting. It had great returns in years one through three, one bad year in year four, and another good year in year five. Which fund would you see profiled on CNBC and *Money* magazine? Obviously, it would be the Exciting Fund; not many people would care much about the Boring Fund. Without peaking, which fund do you think would have made the most money?

The Boring Fund. If you had invested $100,000 into each, at the end of five years you would have $140,255 in the Boring Fund and $130,680 in the Exciting Fund. The Boring Fund shareholders would have been almost $10,000 richer and would have had a much smoother ride. The reason for this is the one year the Exciting Fund had a large loss wiped out most of the performance. To understand this better, you need to understand the math of the markets. Let's say you lose 50 percent on a stock or mutual fund. How much do you have to earn percentage wise just to break even? The answer is 100 percent.

So the first rule of making money in the market is that, if you can avoid large losses, you don't need large gains. The only reason investors needed to be up 28 percent in 2003 was to try to recoup some of their losses from 2000–2002. It may seem like everyone should know this rule but they don't. If you are constantly chasing hot performance, trying to guess what direction the market is going, and buying things on hot tips, you will eventually have a large loss.

Long-Term Time Horizon

If we look at every one-year period in the market from 1926–2005, we find that 71 percent of the time the market has been up, and 29 percent of the time, the market has been down. If we look at every five-year period in the market during the same period, we find that 90 percent of the time the market is up, and 10 percent of the time the market is down. We have had only two negative ten-year periods in the market, both during the Depression, and we have never had a negative fifteen-year period in the market. What does that tell you about the market? It tells you that you need to have a long-term time horizon. Whenever anyone asks me what I think the market is going to do, I say that ten years from now it will be up. My wealthy grandparents didn't try to outguess the market; they invested for the long term.

When you think of the top investors of all time, names like Peter Lynch and Warren Buffet invariably come up. Both of these men have often been quoted saying they have no idea of the short-term direction of the stock market.

So if the three brightest investment minds in our country, Peter Lynch, Warren Buffet, and Matthew Tuttle (OK, so maybe I don't deserve to be mentioned in the same sentence with those guys, but you can't blame me for trying) don't know what the market is going to do, nobody does.

People get confused about the market because the stock market knows nothing about the short term. We see newspaper headlines that scream gloom and doom and then see that the stock market is up that day. Or we see headlines about how great the economy is doing and the market is down that day, and we can't understand it. I remember one day in 2005 when the market was up 150 points, and the commentators were all saying that it was because of a drop in oil prices. The next day oil prices declined, but the market went down 150 points. If that's not enough to confuse you, I don't know what is.

If you look at it in large chunks of time, it makes perfect sense. Over time, the economy has grown and the market has gone up. Trying to figure out what the market will do in the short term is purely guesswork, so stop worrying about it and adopt a long-term time horizon.

I know what you are thinking. In the beginning of the book, I said that when you are retired you don't have a long time to recover from mistakes, and now I am saying you should have a long-term time horizon. Which is it? Well, it's both. That brings me to the third thing you need to know. You must have some method of investing that takes your emotions out of the equation. My wealthy grandparents had a methodology, while my poor grandparents didn't.

Methodology

We have already ascertained that over long periods of time the market has done well. Individual investors lose money because they let their emotions dictate their buy and sell decisions. Your emotions cause you to get greedy and buy something you shouldn't buy, and your emotions cause you to panic and sell something you shouldn't sell. You may read the newspaper and see headlines about how the market went down a hundred points, and you panic and sell. Or you may read magazines like *BusinessWeek*. Here's what *BusinessWeek* said about the stock market in 1979:

For better or worse then the U.S. Economy probably has to regard the death of equities as a near permanent condition. The old attitude of buying solid stocks as a cornerstone for one's life savings and retirement has simply disappeared.

BusinessWeek "The Death of Equities" August 13, 1979

This is the financial industry's equivalent to Dewey defeats Truman: totally and completely wrong. So don't read the magazines, don't read the newspapers, and don't listen to the talking heads on TV. Or, if you do, take it all with a grain of salt. Don't use what you see or read to decide your investment strategy.

Think about it, have you ever felt like you had an investment curse? Right after you buy something, it goes down and right after you sell, it goes up? When I pose this question in one of my speeches, I get a lot of nods. This squiggly line is why that happens.

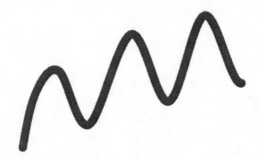

No investment I have ever seen goes up or down in a straight line. It usually goes in a squiggly pattern like the one above. Now think about how most investments are sold. You either buy a mutual fund that is advertised in the paper or in a magazine, or you buy a stock recommended by your broker. Have you ever seen a mutual fund advertisement that said this fund was down 25 percent last year so now is a good time to buy? I doubt it; the advertising firm would probably get fired. You usually see an ad saying that a fund was up 25 percent last year, so it must be a great place to put your money. Does your broker usually call you about a stock that has gone down, or does he call you about a stock that has gone up? Usually, the broker is going to call about a stock that has been appreciating. Therefore, as an individual investor, you are usually buying investments when they are up, and then your emotions cause you to panic, and you sell them when they go down.

Here's a good example of that: *Money* magazine did an interesting study in 1996. They selected five top-performing funds and looked at how the average shareholder did with them. Here's what they found:

	Fund	Shareholders
Dreyfus Aggressive Growth	20.7	-34.9
Hancock Discovery B	13.1	-3.0
Midas Fund	21.2	-14.5
PBHG Core Growth	32.8	-3.0
Van Wagoner Emer. Growth	26.9	-20.0

The fund columns show the annualized return reported by the fund. The shareholder column shows the shareholder average return. The difference results because the average investor invests once the fund has risen (near the top) and then gets out when the fund declines. This is not always the case and is merely an example of what occurred in these funds as reported by Money *magazine during this period. Source:* Money *magazine April 1997. Comparison of fund reported results 12/31/95 to 12/31/96 vs. average investor results (investor results as measured by actual investor accounts in these funds during this period and then averaged). Hancock Discovery B is now Hancock large cap growth B.*

So, for example, the Dreyfus Aggressive growth fund was up 20.7 percent in 1996, but the average shareholder lost 34.9 percent that year. How could this be? Was it an accounting scandal? Was it Enron? Think back to the squiggly line. The Dreyfus fund didn't go up in a straight line all throughout 1996; it went up and down, up and down. To get a 20.7 percent return, you would have had to buy the fund on January 1 and hold it until December 31, but that's not what the average shareholder did. The average shareholder probably saw an ad when the fund started the year well and bought it when it was high. Inevitably during the year the fund must have taken a dip. The average shareholder panicked and sold on the dip.

Developing a methodology involves having a written plan for how you will invest, what you will invest in, when you will buy, and when you will sell. Your written plan dictates all investment decisions (not your emotions or the headlines), and the plan is only altered if changes in your financial situation necessitate it. So how do you develop your methodology?

There are a number of methodologies that work: the Dow Dividend Strategy, CANSLIM, the Value Line Strategy, American Association of Individual Investors, modern portfolio theory, and core-satellite are a few. If you have an advisor, he or she likely has their own strategy. You can use a system that already exists or develop your own. The next chapter will explain the philosophy that makes the most sense when it comes to investing your money—Goals-Based Investing.

Conclusion

To recap, there are three things that will substantially improve your chances of successfully investing: avoid large losses, have a long-term time horizon, and have some sort of system that takes your emotions out of the equation. What the talking heads on CNBC are saying or the hot tip from your broker or neighbor has a much lower chance of achieving success.

Action Plan

1. In chapter 4 you organized your finances. (You did do that didn't you?) Get out your investment, IRA, and 401(k) statements and look at them.

2. Be honest with yourself. Was there an investment strategy that went into the selection of your investments, or do they look like the clutter in your attic? Don't get emotional about your investments. Put your emotions about individual investments aside. Yes, I know you are convinced that a certain stock or fund will go up, but that doesn't affect the chances that it will.

3. Don't beat yourself up over past mistakes; learn from them and focus on the future. We all should have bought Microsoft when it first came out, but we didn't. It's time to move on.

4. If you are completely comfortable with your investments and investment strategy, that's fine. If not, you will need to make some changes. The third section of the book will help you decide if you want to do it yourself or get help.

CHAPTER 6

GOALS-BASED INVESTING

Author's note: I aim to keep things as simple as possible. In parts of this chapter, I delve into some complex issues in portfolio management and structure. For those of you working with an investment professional, it is not important that you understand all of the concepts in this chapter; as it is hoped that your advisor will. For those of you who are committed to doing it yourself, I hope you enjoy some of the concepts and discussion.

Modern portfolio theory (MPT) is perhaps the most widely accepted investment philosophy today. It involves using a complicated process to determine the appropriate allocation of your assets between large stocks, small stocks, international stocks, bonds, and so forth. MPT was originally designed as a way for large institutions to invest their money, but, during the eighties and nineties, individual investors started adopting it as well. MPT has one major flaw: it assumes that all investors behave rationally. During the bull market of the eighties and nineties, it was easy to overlook this flaw, as everyone was making truckloads of money. The decline of 2000–2002 and the subsequent market uncertainty highlighted this issue and started an entirely new field of study called behavioral finance. With the understanding that individual investors didn't behave rationally, behavioral finance practitioners sought to understand how they actually did behave. This study found the following:

	Traditional MPT View of Market Risks and Goals	Individual Investor's Actual View of Risks and Goals
Objective	• Seek performance in line with the markets	• Achieve goal • Protect against loss • Generate income • Growth
Risk Measure	• Standard deviation • Risk relative to benchmark	• Risk of loss • Risk of not meeting goal
Return Measure	• Annualized return • Cumulative return	• Reaching target goal value • Absolute return • Stable return stream • Stable cash flow
Reference Point	• Return relative to benchmark	• High water mark • Goal attainment

Objective

The traditional view of investing was to always beat or match some benchmark. This was played out in the whole argument over whether it was better to buy index funds and match the return of the market or buy actively managed funds to try to beat the market. Beating or matching the market, however, is irrelevant (and perhaps dangerous) if you don't achieve your goals. Assume that you are fifty-five and your goal is to retire at sixty-five, and you want me to design a plan to get you there. Now it's ten years later, and I have some good news and some bad news for you. The good news is that over the ten years the market averaged 6 percent per year and your portfolio averaged 7 percent per year; we beat the market. The bad news is that you still have to work another ten years until you can retire. Are you happy? You beat the market, but you are nowhere near reaching your goal.

Another objective that individual investors have is to protect against loss no matter what the market does. Assume you walk into my office in 2000 with $1 million to invest. I come back to you at the end of 2002 again with some good news and bad news. Your portfolio is now worth $700,000; we lost $300,000, but we beat the market over that period. Are you happy? I doubt it.

As a retiree you might also want to generate income to maintain your lifestyle. You need a certain amount coming in every month, regardless of what the market does.

Risk Measure

The traditional view of investing measures risk by either standard deviation or risk relative to a benchmark like the S&P 500. Unfortunately, most individual investors do not know what standard deviation means. Let's say you are a client of mine, and again I have some good news and bad news. The bad news is that your portfolio lost $100,000 this month. The good news is that the overall standard deviation of the portfolio is only four. Are you happy with that? Again, I doubt it.

When individual investors think about risk, they think about the risk of losing money or the risk of not achieving their goal. Nobody has ever asked me what the standard deviation of their investment portfolio was.

Return Measure

The traditional view looks at return as annualized or cumulative return. While individual investors look at those numbers, they only tell part of the story. Individual investors also look at their progress toward their goals, absolute return, whether they lost any money, a stable return stream, and/or a stable cash flow.

I believe that this decade will be the decade of absolute return. Investors won't care as much about trying to match or beat the market; they will be more concerned with beating zero, or beating what they could earn on a short-term CD. That is what our firm is concerned with. We don't care about beating the market; we just don't want to lose money.

How the market does is irrelevant (or should be) to the individual. Progress should be measured by how close you are to achieving your goal. Think about it; if your goal is to generate $50,000 per year (indexed for inflation) for the rest of your life, does it really matter what your investments are doing in the market if you are able to achieve your goal?

Reference Point

The traditional view uses return vs. a benchmark as the reference point. Individual investors look at goal attainment. Individual investors also look at the high water mark of their portfolio. For example, let's say you came to me with $1 million in 1995. By the end of 1999, let's assume your portfolio had grown to $2 million. Are you happy with that? Who wouldn't be happy about doubling their money? Now let's say that at the end of 2002 your portfolio had declined to $1.5 million. How do you look at that? Do you look at the fact that you started with $1 million and gained $500,000 over seven years or do you look at the fact that you had $2 million and you lost $500,000? Most individual investors look at this as a loss of $500,000. They use the high water mark, in this case $2 million, as their reference point for gains and losses.

Goals-Based Investing

Understanding that individual investors don't behave rationally means that we can do one of two things: we can try to educate individuals to behave rationally (like how my wife tries to educate me to put the toilet seat down, take out the garbage, and mow the lawn), or we could design portfolios for the way investors actually behave. Since I believe in taking the path of least resistance, I believe in designing portfolios for the way you actually think. Goals-Based Investing, which was developed by SEI Investments, does that.

Goals-Based Investing rests upon two key tenets:
1. You have unique goals and objectives.
2. Each goal requires a unique portfolio.

The traditional way to manage money involves figuring out a client's risk tolerance and her needed or expected portfolio return, then creating a diversified portfolio. While this approach is valid, it has a number of limitations.
1. It assumes that you have one risk input, meaning you either prefer low, medium, or high risk. How individuals think about risk, however, tends to be dependent on their goal—for example, the risk you would be willing to take if your goal was to generate income to fund your lifestyle would probably be drastically different from the risk you were willing to take if you were saving up to buy a boat.
2. Traditional theory assumes that all goals have the same priority and time frame. This is not true. Some goals are more important

than others and can have vastly different time horizons. Because goals have different time frames and priorities, different portfolios for each goal may be warranted.

Constructing Goals-Based Portfolios is a five-step process:

Step 1: Define and categorize your goals. If you did the goal-setting exercise earlier in the book, then you have a list of your goals. If not, go back to chapter 2 and do the exercise. As you remember from chapter 2, your goals generally fall into one of four categories: want to now, want to later, have to now, and have to later.

Want to Now Goals:	Want to Later Goals:	Have to Now Goals:	Have to Later Goals:
Short time horizon	Long time horizon	Short time horizon	Long time horizon
Low priority	Low priority	High priority	High priority

Goals-Based Investing would have a different portfolio for each of these types of goals. For example, if your have-to-now goal is to fund your current lifestyle, the objectives for this portfolio may be to protect against market declines and allow you to maintain your spending level. On the other hand a want-to-later goal might be to save enough money to buy a boat. The objectives for this portfolio may be to aggressively grow assets for the long term. Once your goals have been identified, you must figure out how much resources you have to allocate to each goal. This is also where prioritization comes into play; it is possible that you will not have enough resources to fund all of your goals.

Traditional Approach   Goals-Based Approach

One portfolio	→ Goal 1	**Goal 1 Portfolio**	**Goal 2 Portfolio**	**Goal 3 Portfolio**
One risk tolerance	→ Goal 2	Risk tolerance for goal	Risk tolerance for goal	Risk tolerance for goal
Success determined by performance vs. market	→ Goal 3	Success determined by progress toward goal	Success determined by progress toward goal	Success determined by progress toward goal

The traditional approach has one portfolio and one risk tolerance, and success is determined by performance vs. the market. This one portfolio is expected to meet the needs of each goal. The goals-based approach has one portfolio for each goal, one risk tolerance for each goal, and success is determined by progress toward the goal.

Different Goals Have Different Strategies

Goal	Portfolio Objective	Strategy
Maintain current lifestyle	Competitive return/ control risk of loss	Stability focused
Future retirement	Competitive returns while protecting portfolio value at retirement date	Time focused
Leave pool of money to children—Legacy	Competitive returns while controlling risk vs. the market	Market focused
"Fun money"	Aggressive returns	Growth focused

The goals-based approach increases the likelihood of achieving your goals and manages the limitations of traditional investment theory, since there is no longer one risk input.

Risks and Challenges

For every goal that you have, there will be certain risks and challenges that threaten its achievement.

Here is an example:

Life Goals	Real Risks and Challenges
Current Lifestyle	Have I saved enough? Do I have enough for my current lifestyle? Will unexpected expenses derail my other goals?
Charitable Contributions	What if I don't have enough to contribute?
Vacation Home	What if I don't have enough money to buy another vacation home? What if I don't grow my money aggressively enough?
Retire at Sixty-Five Years of Age	Can I afford to take on new hobbies or travel as much as I would like to? Will my spouse want to retire before me or after me? What if I can't work to sixty-five? What if the cost of my lifestyle increases?

Exercise: Take the goals you listed in chapter 2 and categorize them by want to now, want to later, have to now, and have to later. Then write down all of the challenges and risks you can think of for each goal.

Here's an example:

Have to Now Goals:

Generate $50,000/year indexed for inflation every year for the rest of my life.

Risks and Challenges:

Market downturn, higher than expected inflation, health-care crisis, higher expenses, $50,000/year too low.

Now list your goals from chapter 2:

Want to Now Goals: **Risks and Challenges:**	**Want to Later Goals:** **Risks and Challenges:**
Have to Now Goals: **Risks and Challenges:**	**Have to Later Goals:** **Risks and Challenges:**

Step 2: Assessment and Evaluation. Now that you know your goals, the next step is to define your overall risk tolerance. The exercise below will help you determine a risk tolerance score:

Instructions: For each question, circle the number after the answer that is most appropriate. If you are doing this exercise with your partner, then both of you should circle an answer and average your scores.

1. When you think of the word *risk* in a financial context, which of the following words comes to mind first?	Score 1	Score 2
A. Thrill	5	5
B. Uncertainty	3	3
C. Opportunity	3	3
D. Danger	1	1
2. What is your greatest concern?		
A. Underperforming the market	5	5
B. Not growing my assets significantly over time: I am willing to assume higher risk for higher return potential	5	5
C. Losing more than a certain amount within a time frame	3	3
D. Losing money in a market downturn along the way	3	3
E. Not having certainty around achieving my wealth goal in the remaining time	1	1
3. If the market falls by 25 percent in a year, and you lose 20 percent, how do you feel?		
A. Optimistic because I beat the market by thinking long term	5	5
B. Uneasy with loss but I stick it out	3	3
C. Unhappy with the loss to the point where I will sell	1	1
4. What describes you best?		
A. I am long-term focused	5	5
B. I am focused on preserving current wealth and have little tolerance for losses	3	3
C. I want to plan long term but have a hard time shrugging off moderate to severe losses	3	3
D. I am most concerned about targeting a final value of my assets: I don't mind if this approach sacrifices return potential.	1	1
5. If I look at my quarterly statement and there is a moderate loss, my primary reaction is:		
A. How did my portfolio compare with the market benchmark or other relative measures of success?	5	5

B. I lost money and am unhappy but am willing to stick it through until a recovery	3	3
C. I don't care about short-term losses as long as I reach a specific sum of money at a specific point of time in the future	1	1
Overall Risk Score(s)		
Average Risk Score (if scoring with partner)		

Source: SEI Investments

Risk Tolerance Scoring Guide

After adding your scores from the questionnaire, you have a total risk tolerance score. This score will provide some guidance in choosing the appropriate investment strategies for each of your goals. Please keep in mind that a risk tolerance questionnaire is just a tool and has its limitations. Always use your own judgment or seek the help of a financial planning professional.

Score

5–11   Low: choose conservative/low-risk strategies

12–17   Moderate: choose moderate/medium-risk strategies

18–25   High: choose aggressive/high-risk strategies

Step 3: Implementation. Now that you know your goals and your overall risk tolerance, the next step is implementing your strategy.

Diversification

Diversification is spreading your portfolio among different types of investments with the hope that the investments not performing well during a specific period are balanced off by the investments that are performing well, resulting in more consistent returns. The bear market of 2000–2002 reinforced this idea, with investors concentrated in growth or technology stocks taking a beating while those with well-diversified portfolios came out much better. The underpinning of any goals-based strategy is proper diversification.

Goals-Based Portfolios

There are four primary types of portfolios that are appropriate for a goals-based approach: stability focused, time focused, market focused, and aggressive growth.

Portfolio Type	Client's View	Goal Examples
Stability Focused	I don't want to lose money	Maintain lifestyle, retirement in near term
Time Focused	I need to have x$	College costs, retirement
Market Focused	Keeping up	Leaving a Legacy
Aggressive Growth	Home run	Fun money

First, you must apply your overall risk tolerance score to each category of goals as follows:

Want to Now Goals	Want to Later Goals
Objective: Grow Assets	Objective: Grow Assets
Strategy Suggestions:	Strategy Suggestions:
Risk Tolerance:	Risk Tolerance:
Low **Moderate** **High**	**Low** **Moderate** **High**
Growth & Market Aggressive Income Growth Growth	Growth & Market Aggressive Income Growth Growth Market Aggressive Growth Growth

Have to Now Goals	Have to Later Goals
Objective: Protect against losses, maintain steady growth	Objective: Preserve a guaranteed sum, have enough when the time comes
Strategy Suggestions:	Strategy Suggestions:
Risk Tolerance:	Risk Tolerance:
Low **Moderate** **High**	**Low** **Moderate** **High**
Defensive Conservative Moderate Stability Stability Stability	Defensive Conservative Moderate Stability Stability Stability Time Time Aggressive Focused Focused Growth

So for example, if you have a have-to-now goal and a low tolerance for risk, a defensive strategy may be appropriate.

Below are some examples of portfolios that could be appropriate for each type of goal.

(Author's note: The following example portfolios are just that—examples; please remember that past performance doesn't predict future results. You are always better off going to a professional for advice. I put the example portfolios in as an educational tool and a framework for those die-hard do-it-yourselfers.)

Stability Portfolios

Stability-focused portfolios are appropriate for have-to goals since you generally cannot afford large losses or volatility in goals that you must have. Diversification is the key to stability. Diversification means not putting all of your eggs in one basket and is the best way to manage the risks you identified for your goals. Since different types of investments have different risk and return characteristics, you must effectively diversify to meet the risk and return needs of your goal. Because you are trying to reach a goal regardless of what the market does, stability is key. Studies have determined that selected asset classes exist, such as short duration bonds, investment-grade bonds, high-yield, REITs, and U.S. large cap value, that have more stable returns over time than the more volatile asset classes, such as U.S. small cap, international equity, commodities, and U.S. large cap growth (see the chart below). This market value stability is critically important, especially if you are retired and withdrawing assets from the pool. The main component of stability-based portfolios is short-term bonds because they have the lowest potential loss of all the other components. Other assets in the portfolio have higher potential returns. By combining short-term bonds with these return-enhancing vehicles, we can achieve a balance between risk control and growth. This will help you avoid large losses and will help you look for funds more like the Boring Fund than the Exciting Fund.

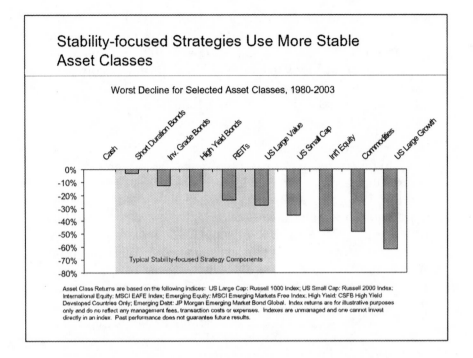

Special Asset Classes to Consider with Stability Portfolios

In addition to the asset classes I mentioned above, there are a number of other types of investments that don't fit neatly into a Morningstar-style box for stability portfolios:

Floating Rate Funds: These funds buy floating rate bank loans. Unlike normal bonds that pay a fixed rate of interest, these bank loans float, so if interest rates rise the loans pay a higher rate. This provides bank loans some stability in a rising rate environment but not in a falling rate environment. You should also note that bank loans are not as liquid as bonds, and the underlying loans generally have a low credit quality.

Long/Short Funds: These funds buy stocks of companies they like and sell short stocks of companies they do not like. Short selling is the process of selling stock that you don't own and hoping to buy it back later at a lower price. For example, let's say I think the stock of XYZ is selling at $560 per share, and I believe it is overpriced. I could borrow 100 shares from my stock broker and sell them, netting $5,000 ($50 × 100). A month later, let's assume that XYZ has declined to $40 per share. I can buy back my 100 shares for $4,000 ($40 × 100) and give them back to my broker. I get to keep the $1,000 profit. Of course if I am wrong and XYZ goes up in value, then I will have to buy the shares back at a higher price. A long/short fund will use these strategies to attempt to profit in any market.

Merger Arbitrage Funds: These funds buy stocks of companies involved in announced mergers. For example, let's assume that Coke decides they are going to buy Pepsi in three months. Let's also assume that Pepsi is trading at $40 per share before the announcement, and Coke is offering to buy all shares for $50 per share. Pepsi will immediately go up in value, but it won't go to $50 per share, since there are three months until the deal closes and anything can happen during that time. Pepsi might go up to $49.50 per share. A merger arbitrage fund would buy Pepsi at $49.50 and hold it for three months when it collects $50 per share. A merger arbitrage fund will keep doing this throughout the year, hoping to make small profits on a number of deals.

Funds That Allow the Portfolio Manager to Hedge His/Her Bets: There are some funds that give the portfolio manager the flexibility to hedge his or her bets by using options and futures during a down market.

Commodity-Linked Funds: These funds are generally linked to some sort of index of commodities and are generally heavily weighted toward oil.

Hedge Funds or Hedge Fund of Funds: When people think of hedge funds, they tend to think high risk. While there are some hedge funds that do take large risks, others don't. Hedge funds employ a number of different strategies, including some of the ones above, and can help reduce the risk of an overall portfolio. Individual investors might be better off with a fund of funds in which a manager picks a number of different hedge funds for you to spread out the risk.

These Types of Investments Can Help You Plan for the Worst and Hope for the Best

There are four bad things that can happen to your portfolio: stock prices could go down, interest rates could go up, inflation could go up, or oil prices could go up. Instead of trying to forecast when or if these events will occur, we must plan for them ahead of time. We will always include at least one mutual fund in every client's portfolio that should go up if the market goes down, should go up if interest rates go up, should go up if inflation goes up, and should go up if oil prices go up. That way we don't care what happens in the market, the economy, or the world because we have prepared for almost anything.

My philosophy is to control what I can and not worry about what I can't. Spending time trying to figure out if the market is going to go up or down or which way interest rates are going is an exercise in futility. We have no control over these events; the only thing we can control is risk. The market will either go up or it won't, the logical thing to do is to be prepared either way.

This type of strategy will not be for everybody. Since we are prepared for the worst, if the best happens we should still do fine but not as well as someone who didn't prepare for the downside. Unfortunately, you cannot have your cake and eat it too.

Stability-Focused Strategies:

Defensive Stability: Risk control takes precedence over growth of assets

Investment	%
Ultra Short Term Bond	64%
Investment Grade Bond	10%
High Yield Bond	10%
U.S. Stock	10%
Real Estate	5%
Cash/Money Market	1%

Conservative Stability: A balance of growth and risk control

Investment	%
Ultra Short Term Bond	44%
Investment Grade Bond	10%
High Yield Bond	15%
U.S. Stock	20%
Real Estate	10%
Cash/Money Market	1%

Moderate Stability: An emphasis on growth with a secondary objective of controlling risk.

Investment	%
Ultra Short Term Bond	19%
Investment Grade Bond	20%
High Yield Bond	15%
U.S. Stock	30%
International Stock	5%
Real Estate	10%
Cash/Money Market	1%

In taxable accounts (non-IRAs), the ultra short-term bonds and investment-grade bonds should be municipal. In non-taxable accounts (IRAs, 401(k)s, etc), they could be corporate bonds, mortgage backed bonds, government bonds, and so on.

Stability-Focused Strategy Components

Component	Role In Strategy
Short-Term Bonds	Provides a low-risk anchor with returns in excess of money markets.
Investment-Grade Bonds	Provides higher return potential than short-term bonds with less risk than stocks.
High-Yield Bonds	Provides higher return potential than investment-grade bonds with less risk than stocks.
U.S. Stock	Higher return potential than bonds.
International Stock	Adds to diversification.
REITs	Adds to diversification.

Market-Focused Strategies

Growth and Income: An emphasis on growth while maintaining stock & bond market participation.

Type of Investment	%
Investment Grade Bond	49%
High Yield Bond	5%
U.S. Stock	30%
International Stock	9%
Emerging Market Stock	1%
Emerging Market Bond	5%
Cash	1%

Market Growth: An emphasis on growth while maintaining stock and bond market participation.

Type of Investment	%
Investment Grade Bond	25%
High Yield Bond	8%
U.S. Stock	44%
International Stock	13%
Emerging Market Stock	2%
Emerging Market Bond	7%
Cash	1%

Aggressive Growth: Maximum growth over long-term time horizons

Type of Investment	%
High Yield Bond	9%
U.S. Stock	60%
International Stock	18%
Emerging Market Stock	2%
Emerging Market Bond	10%
Cash	1%

In taxable accounts (non-IRAs), the ultra short-term bonds and investment-grade Bonds should be municipal. In non-taxable accounts (IRAs, 401(k)s, etc) they could be corporate bonds, mortgage backed bonds, government bonds, and so on.

Time-Focused Strategy

Time-focused strategies are used when the investor wants growth but needs a minimum guaranteed portfolio value at some point in the future. The best way is to use a type of bond known as a zero coupon bond. Most bonds pay interest every year and then pay back the principal of the bond at maturity. A zero coupon bond pays no interest and is sold at a deep discount to its payoff value. For example, let's assume that I know that I need $100 in five years. I could find a zero coupon bond that would allow me to put down less than $100 (the amount would depend on interest rates at the time and some other more complex factors) and would guarantee (based on the bond issuer's ability to pay the claim) that they would pay me $100 in five years. That would be a low/no risk way to guarantee that I would have my $100 when I needed it. I could also take a little risk to attempt to add some return; I could buy a zero coupon bond that would guarantee me $50 in five years and put the rest of my money into the market for a potentially higher return (there are no guarantees of course). Here's an example. Let's assume that I need $1 million in ten years, and I have $500,000 today. Let's also assume that I could put $350,000 into a zero coupon bond that would guarantee me $700,000 in ten years. I could then take the remaining $150,000 and invest it aggressively, knowing that I would have at least $700,000 in ten years.

Here's an example of a time-focused strategy with 100 percent protection:

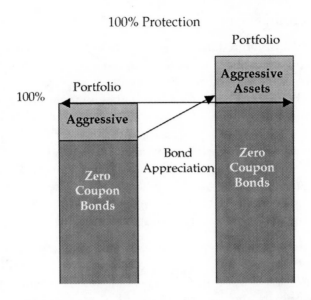

In this example, we invest enough in zero coupon bonds to ensure that our portfolio will be at least what we started with at our goal date. The rest is invested aggressively in hope of potentially increasing the portfolio value.

How Much to Put in Each Portfolio

Once you know your goals and how you want to invest your assets, the next step is to determine how much to allocate toward each goal. You will need some sort of time value of money calculator. If you are Microsoft Excel literate, this can simply be time value of money Excel calculations in which you enter how much you have now, how much you need, when, and at what rate you expect the assets to grow (for a rate you might want to pick something conservative like 5–7 percent). A number of calculators are also available on the Internet, and of course your financial advisor should be able to do these calculations for you.

Tax Management

Taxes can have a large negative effect on your portfolio. It's not the money you earn that matters; it's the money you keep.

Picking Mutual Funds and/or Money Managers

The final implementation step is picking the actual mutual funds and/or money managers to manage the different parts of your portfolio. Again, this is a very complex process and not for the faint of heart. Picking money managers and monitoring them takes work. If you are not willing to do that, then please get the help of a professional. For the remainder of this discussion, when I use the term *money manager*, I am referring to mutual funds or separately managed accounts. I will not talk about individual stocks or bonds here. They can be perfectly valid for a goals-based approach but require much more time and expertise to choose and monitor.

Here is the process we use to evaluate and choose money managers; if you are doing this on your own, you will need access to some sort of mutual fund database like Morningstar. A less-sophisticated approach might be to select one or two fund companies with a broad line up of funds that you can research in depth.

Here's how we do it:

- **Criteria**: The first thing we must do is define what type of manager we are looking for: large cap value, small cap growth, international, and so on.
- **Philosophy**: We look for specialist money managers who have a clearly defined investment philosophy and style, such as large stocks and international stocks, that has been consistently applied over a large number of years.
- **Discipline**: We then note how the firms put the philosophy into action and make sure there is some sort of discipline regarding decisions (similar to how we recommend individuals have a specific investment methodology).
- **Consistency**: We compare the manager's performance against the relevant benchmarks to determine whether their performance is consistent with their investment process and what we would expect.
- **Talent**: When you hire a money manager you would prefer someone who is talented and good at what they do. We look for firms that are well managed and able to attract and retain

the best investment talent. We prefer a team approach to managing money instead of relying on one star manager.

- **Money Managers Who Put Their Money Where Their Mouth Is:** We believe that you should invest with money managers who put their money in their own funds. It always amazes me how a fund can say how great it is, but the money manager won't put any of his or her own money in it. If I was managing a mutual fund and I had confidence in my investment skill, why wouldn't I put my own money in my fund?

  If you remember back to the mutual fund scandals of the past few years, they were by and large committed by people who didn't have their own money in their funds. If you had a substantial amount of money in your fund, would you commit a crime to the detriment of shareholders? Probably not.

  The last reason why I think this is important is that if a portfolio manager has a lot of money in their own fund, they will care even more than I do if it is down.

- **Good at Managing Money, Bad at Marketing:** We look for companies good at managing money but who don't put a lot of time or money in marketing themselves. There is only so much money a mutual fund can handle. Even the best mutual fund manager can have too much money to invest. Mutual funds that have large positions in stocks can also have a hard time buying and selling without moving the market against them. For these reasons, we prefer smaller funds that nobody has heard of. Once the public hears about a good fund, they pour money into it, which can hurt the fund's performance.

- **Fit:** We might find a great manager, but she may be very similar to an existing manager we already use. We would rather find managers whose performance is not in line with other managers we are using. This is called correlation; we are looking for managers who have a low correlation with each other.

Step 4: Monitoring. Once you have diversified and chosen your investments, you must monitor them constantly to make sure they are performing as you would expect and are consistent with their style. For example, if you have a fund that invests in small stocks, you want to make sure that it isn't drifting into larger stocks. There are a number of events that could cause you to consider replacing managers:

- A change in the stability of the organization or turnover of employees
- Poor performance
- The manager is growing too fast (i.e., they might be great at managing $100 million but can they manage $1 billion?)
- A better manager for that slot is discovered

Step 5: Track your progress. Track your progress toward your goals. If your goal is to generate $50,000 per year in income and to grow the portfolio to keep pace with inflation, how did you do or how are you doing relative to your goal?

Here is an example of the simple tracking method we employ:

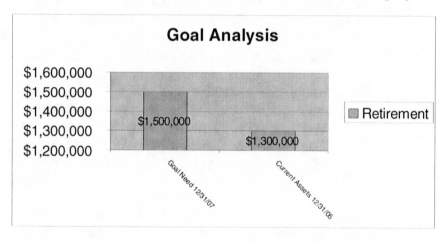

Here is a case study that gives an example of the Goals-Based Investing process:

Investors: Tom and Mary Jones

Investment Assets: $1 million investment portfolio

Goals: To support lifestyle in retirement (have to now) by generating an extra $38,000 from the portfolio and to travel the world (want to later).

Goal 1: Lifestyle in Retirement (Have to Now)

Biggest Risks: Running out of money or reducing lifestyle

Objective: To protect against loss and maintain spending level

Maintaining Spending Levels to Withdraw What Is Needed:

Investor will not be able to withstand substantial market volatility, especially on the downside, because the investor will not be able to withdraw enough money from his account.

Solution: A protective strategy can provide more growth than a 100 percent bond strategy (see table 6) and more downside protection than a traditional stock/bond mix.

Protective Strategy Example:

Ultra Short Bond	44%
Core Bond	10%
High-Yield Bond	15%
Real Estate	10%
Managed Volatility Stock*	20%
Cash	1%

*Managed volatility portfolio managers invest in stocks but use hedging techniques to reduce risk.

SEI GoalLink Conservative Strategy Portfolio as of 7/5/06. This portfolio is an example only.

With a withdrawal rate of 4 percent per year, $950,000 invested in the protective strategy would generate $38,000. We will talk more about withdrawals in chapter 7. Progress would be measured by success or failure in generating the required income while growing enough to meet future inflation.

Protective Strategies Provide Better Defense than U.S. Bonds (for illustrative purposes only)

$600,000 Invested on January 1, 1966
1966–1981 (high inflationary environment)
Includes 4 Percent Annual Drawdown Rate, Adjusted for Inflation

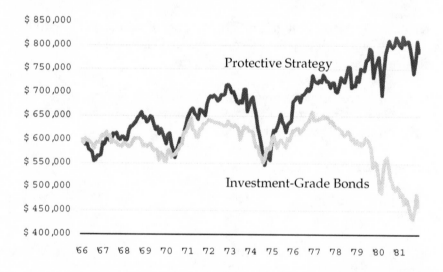

The difference between the protective strategy and the investment-grade bonds is $328,000.

In high-inflation environments, the protective strategy, which is representative of SEI's stability-focused moderate strategy, provides growth while the 100 percent bond strategy begins to deteriorate.

Does not represent actual SEI strategy performance. Results are based on market index returns weighted according to November 2004 strategy weights and without tax management or hedge funds. Source: SEI Investments and market data from Ibbotson Associates. Investment-grade bonds = Ibbotson US Intermediate Term Government 1966–1972. Lehman US Government/Corporate Index 1973–1975. Lehman US Aggregate Bond Index, 1976–1981

The time period 1966–1981 was chosen because it is indicative of a high-inflationary environment. The 4 percent annual drawdown rate is indicative of a client's typical drawdown rate. The inflation assumption is ~3 percent, based on SEI research.

Goal 2: Traveling the World (Want to Later)

Objective: To aggressively grow assets to achieve maximum return

As this goal is not a current requirement, the investor has the flexibility to invest aggressively to achieve the highest maximum return possible and can withstand significant risk as a result.

As per the investor's goals, a strategy that seeks to achieve maximum return would be appropriate for this goal.

Aggressive Strategy Example:

Large Cap Diversified	48%
International Stock	18%
Emerging Market Bond	10%
High-Yield Bond	9%
Small Cap Value	6%
Small Cap Growth	6%
Emerging Market Stock	2%
Cash	1%

SEI GoalLink Aggressive Strategy Portfolio as of 7/5/06. This portfolio is an example only.

For these investors, $50,000 should be invested in the Aggressive Strategy. Progress would be measured against the market since the goal is to grow this money to the largest possible pool.

Conclusion

I believe that a Goals-Based Investment process aligns your investments with the way you actually think and behave and also gives you the greatest chance of achieving your goals for the reasons that are important to you.

Action Plan:
1. Identify your goals.
2. Identify the relevant risks around each goal.
3. Identify the appropriate portfolio for each goal.
4. Identify the best way to implement that portfolio.

CHAPTER 7

CASH RESERVES

The core of your financial strategy is your cash reserves. By cash reserves I mean money set aside that you can get at in a matter of minutes if you need it in an emergency.

Why you might ask, does a retiree need cash reserves? You may have money in stocks or mutual funds that you can liquidate or perhaps you have interest coming in every month from bonds, so why set aside money in cash? You never know what might happen. If you remember back to the 9/11 crisis, the stock market was shut down for four days. If you needed to sell anything to raise cash, you couldn't have done it. If your investments had been set up to send you a monthly check and the market was closed, that check wouldn't come. Then what would you do? You may not realize it, but mutual funds have a legal right to withhold liquidation requests. That's why you need cash reserves.

How much cash should you reserve? I recommend having three to six months worth of expenses. If you did the exercise in chapter 3, then you know how much cash reserves you should have.

Now that you know how much you should have in cash reserves, where should you put them? First let's go over where not to put cash reserves:

1. Your mattress: Your money earns no interest, and what would happen if your house burned down or you were robbed?

2. CDs: Most CDs have penalties for early withdrawals.

3. Checking accounts: You probably won't earn any interest and might be tempted to use the money.

4. Bonds: Bonds have a fixed maturity date; if you have to sell them before that date, you may get less than you put in.

5. Bond funds: Bond funds have no maturity date and the value can fluctuate day by day.

6. Fixed annuities: Fixed annuities usually have penalties for taking money out early.

    Then where should you put cash reserves? Here are three choices:
1. Money market accounts: These accounts earn interest, and your money is always available by check or ATM card.
2. Savings account: This is the same as a money market account. Make sure the account earns interest.
3. Credit union: Often a credit union will pay a higher interest rate than a bank checking account.

Make sure that whatever you choose you do whatever possible to avoid a fee.

Exercises for Chapter 7:

1.   Record your monthly expenses from chapter 3.

$_____

Multiply by 3.

= $_____
This is the minimum amount you should have in cash reserves.

2.   Compare options:

   A.   Money market

      Interest rate   _____%

      Fees $_____

      Checks   Yes__ No__

      Debit card/ATM   Yes__ No__

B. **Bank savings account**

     Interest rate   _____%

     Fees $_____

     Checks   Yes__ No__

     Debit card/ATM   Yes__ No__

C. **Credit union**

     Interest rate   _____%

     Fees $_____

     Checks   Yes__ No__

     Debit card/ATM   Yes__ No__

Now that your cash reserves are set, the next step is to decide how you will generate income from your portfolio.

CHAPTER 8

TWO WAYS TO CREATE INCOME IN RETIREMENT: HOW MY WEALTHY GRANDPARENTS DID IT AND HOW MY POOR GRANDPARENTS DID IT

Ray came to see me one day. He had been a successful marketing executive and had retired five years ago with a portfolio worth $500,000. When he retired, he had just done what his mother had done; he had invested his money in two bond mutual funds and decided to live off the interest. The funds had been yielding 8 percent, which meant that he had been getting $40,000 a year. That would have been more than enough, but, unfortunately for him, interest rates had started to decline. The financial news had kept saying that interest rates would eventually go up, but the rates had continued to go down. By the time Ray came to see me, his bond funds were yielding 4 percent, and his income had been cut in half. He was now eating into his principal and wasn't sure what he would do if interest rates didn't come back up soon.

Both of my grandmothers retired at about the same age. They both lost their husbands, and they both had about the same amount of money when they retired. My wealthy grandmother had a diversified portfolio from which she took systematic withdrawals. My poor grandmother had the bulk of her money in bonds and lived off the interest. My wealthy grandmother left her children and grandchildren a nice inheritance. My poor grandmother ran out of money. The reason that my poor grandmother's plan didn't work was because of her longevity. She and my grandfather lived much longer than they expected. They lived off a fixed income that did not account for inflation and health-care costs, and they ended up paying the price.

Have you ever been concerned that you will outlive your money? Years ago you worked for one company your whole life and retired at age 65 with a pension, health care coverage, and Social Security. You didn't live that long after retirement so you had nothing to worry about. Well things have changed.

America's financial services industry is doing a good job educating young people on how to accumulate assets: save as early and as often as possible. But for those ready to retire, making the transition from building assets to drawing down their life savings, the stakes rise.

Today's retiree faces five key risks in planning for lifetime income: longevity risk, inflation risk, investment risk, health-care risk, and withdrawal risk.

Longevity Risk

Since 1900, medical science has extended the average life span by thirty-one years! According to the Society of Actuaries, a sixty-five-year-old male now has a 50 percent chance of living to age eighty-five and a 25 percent chance of living to age ninety-two. A sixty-five-year-old female has a 50 percent chance of living to age eighty-eight and 25 percent chance of living to age ninety-four. A sixty-five-year-old couple has a 50 percent chance that one of them will live to age ninety-two. This means that a person retiring at sixty-five might live thirty years or more with no salary coming in, a scary thought isn't it? When planning your lifetime income needs, you need to plan as if you will be around for a long time.

Inflation Risk

Conventional advice is to place all of your money in fixed income investments and live off the interest. That didn't work so well for my grandmother, and it probably won't work so well for you. Because people are living longer, they will have to deal with inflation. For example, let's assume you are a retiree in 2006 who is living on $72,058 a year. At a 3 percent inflation rate, your income need twenty-five years from now will be $150,873, more than double what it is today. Just think what would happen if you put all of your money in fixed income investments generating $72,000 a year. In twenty-five years, they would still be generating that same $72,000. What would you do then? The bad news is that 3 percent may not even be that realistic. A study done by Families USA found that between 1994 and 1999 prices for the fifty most commonly prescribed drugs for older Americans rose 25.2 percent—nearly twice the overall inflation rate for the same five-year period. Because of this, the way my poor grandparents tried to generate income just doesn't work anymore.

Investment Risk

Anyone who had his or her money invested in the stock market from 2000–2002 understands what I am talking about here. The value of the stock market went down more than 40 percent. Because of longevity and inflation, most retirees cannot afford to absorb the kind of market losses we saw during those years. According to a study commissioned by the AARP, among investors age fifty to seventy who lost money in stocks, 76 percent modified their current lifestyle or expectations of their retirement lifestyle. Of those who are not yet retired, one in five has postponed retirement. Of those who are retired, one in ten has returned to work.

This data might suggest that you adopt an ultra-conservative strategy such as investing in CDs or AAA bonds, but remember longevity and inflation risk. This strategy won't keep up with inflation and won't work if you live a long time.

Let's assume we have three investors. Investor number one has a portfolio 100 percent in money market accounts, investor number two has a conservative portfolio of 20 percent stocks, 50 percent bonds, and 30 percent in money market accounts, and investor number three has a portfolio of 50 percent stocks, 40 percent bonds, and 10 percent in money market accounts. Using historical returns on these assets from 1926–2002 and assuming each investor is taking 5 percent (inflation adjusted) of his portfolio out every year for expenses, here is what happens after twenty-five years. Investor number one has a 100 percent chance of running out of money. Investor number two has a 60 percent chance of running out of money. Investor number three has only a 20 percent chance of running out of money.

The bottom line is that stocks must play a major role in your retirement portfolio.

Health-Care Cost Risk

A 2002 study by the Fidelity Employer Services Company estimates that a married couple retiring today at age sixty-five will need current savings of $160,000 to supplement Medicare and cover out-of-pocket health-care costs in retirement, unless they have an employer-funded retirement health plan. Unfortunately, these plans are evaporating fast. In the years from 1995 to 2001, the percentage offering retiree health benefits fell from 35 percent to just 23 percent for companies employing more than 500 workers.

None of these estimates include long-term care expenses, which are covered in detail in the next chapter and could run over $100,000 a year.

Withdrawal Risk

This is the risk of taking too much money out of your portfolio every year. The actual amount you should be withdrawing depends on your age, your health, your needs, and your desire to leave a legacy. During the late nineties, I often met people who had been advised to withdraw 10 percent of their portfolio every year. After all, stocks were increasing by 30 percent a year, so why not?

Generally, I recommend that clients withdraw 4–5 percent per year from a diversified portfolio. Whatever withdrawal rate you choose can have a significant impact on your net worth. Here is an example: suppose you have a portfolio of 50 percent stocks, 40 percent bonds, and 10 percent money markets. The table below shows how long your portfolio would last using withdrawal rates from 4–10 percent and using historical returns from 1926–2002:

Withdrawal rate	Number of years the portfolio may last
10%	11 years
9%	13 years
8%	15 years
7%	18 years
6%	21 years
5%	27 years
4%	33 years

Study done by Fidelity Investments

So for example, if you had $100,000 and took out 4 percent per year, that would equate to $4,000. A 4 percent withdrawal rate does not offer guaranteed retirement security, but it is clear that rates much above that increase the risk that you will outlive your assets.

We don't want to forget about inflation. I recommend you bump up your withdrawals by 3 percent each year to account for inflation. So for example if your year one withdrawal is $100, you will take out $103 in year two, $106.09 in year three, and so on. Of course you don't want to do this in a vacuum. If you are withdrawing more and more from your portfolio each year and it is declining in value, then you will eventually have a problem. You need to evaluate every year how much you are taking out on a percentage basis. If it is much more than 4 percent, you may need to readjust before you run into trouble. So let's say you have $100,000 today and are taking out $4,000 per year. Next year your portfolio goes down by 30 percent; you now have $66,000 ($100,000–30 percent–$4,000). If you take out $4,120 ($4,000 + 3 percent inflation adjustment) that will be 6 percent of your portfolio. Taking 6 percent per year out over an extended period is more risky than 4 percent.

Now I know what some of you might be thinking. If you withdraw 4 percent from your portfolio each year, won't you be eating into some principal? You might, but who cares? Take a dollar out of your pocket and look at it. Is that dollar principal or interest? I bet you can't tell. The last time I looked, it's all green; whether it's principal or interest doesn't matter. So stop getting hung up on principal vs. interest; it will actually help you avoid running out of money.

Action Plan

Step 1: Expenses. What are your expenses? Write down your fixed expenses and your variable expenses from chapter 3:

Fixed Expenses $_____

Variable Expenses $_____

Step 2: Income. List all of your sources of income—Social Security, pensions, and so forth. What assets do you have from chapter 3 that could be used to generate income?

Monthly Income		
	Current	Retirement
Wages, salary, tips		
Cash dividends		
Interest received		
Social Security income		
Pension income		
Rents, royalties		
Other income		
Total Monthly Income		

Growth assets from chapter 3: $_____
4 percent of growth assets = $_____
+
Total monthly income = $_____

= Total income $_____

This is how much income you could generate from your income sources and growth assets.

Step 3: Allocate assets to cover essential expenses and fund discretionary expenses.
Set up a systematic plan to withdraw money from your portfolio to cover any gap between your predictable income and your fixed expenses and to fund your variable expenses. Remember to choose your withdrawal rate carefully. If you have to withdraw more than 4 percent of your portfolio annually to fund the gap, you may need to cut expenses. All things being equal, you should withdraw money

from your taxable accounts first. Leave your IRAs alone as long as possible to continue the tax deferral.

Just about any financial institution should be able to set up a systematic withdrawal plan. Just call and ask for whatever paperwork you need. They can generally wire money into your checking account every month.

At the end of the first year, re-evaluate your withdrawal amount and decide whether or not to increase it 3 percent for inflation.

Step 4: Protect and update the plan. Decide whether to add long-term care and major medical and life insurance to protect your plan. Review your plan at least once a year.

CHAPTER 9

WHAT MY POOR GRANDPARENTS DIDN'T KNOW ABOUT LONG-TERM CARE

Amy came into my office after attending one of my classes and told me straight out that she wanted to purchase long-term care insurance. After talking to her about her finances, I found that she was a widow, she had a liquid net worth of over $6 million dollars, and, while she wanted her children to inherit as much as possible, they were all well off and their inheritance was not a major concern. Even in an expensive state like Connecticut, she would have more than enough money to provide for her care. Before selling her the insurance, I wanted to make sure she clearly understood that. She told me that she did understand. She just wanted the insurance because it would give her peace of mind.

Sue called me one day to talk about long-term care for her and her husband, Ed. She explained that Ed was in early stage Alzheimer's, and she was taking care of him. She asked if I could come by their home since it was difficult for her to leave the house. When I walked in, I saw Ed sitting on the couch. He did not look well. Sue looked like she had not had a good night's sleep in quite a while. I could tell that taking care of Ed was taking a toll on her. We sat down, and she explained that when Ed got sick she did not have enough money to pay someone to come in to take care of him, but she had too much money to qualify for Medicaid. At first she had been able to care for Ed by herself, but now her arthritis was acting up and her eyesight wasn't what it used to be. She didn't know how much longer she could keep going. She asked me if there was any way she could buy long-term care insurance for Ed.

Both of my grandfathers died in their seventies, and both of my grandmothers needed some type of custodial care during their lifetimes. My wealthy grandmother had a home health aide come in to live with her. My poor grandmother ended up in an assisted living facility. One of the biggest reasons my wealthy grandparents died rich and my poor grandparents ran out of money was long-term care insurance. My wealthy grandmother had long-term care insurance, which paid most of the bill for her home health aide. My poor grandmother had left long-term care to chance and had to personally pay the bill for the assisted-living facility.

There is no more contentious issue in financial planning for retirees than long-term care insurance. Why is there such a problem?

Medicare was instituted during the Lyndon Johnson administration. Back then, people did not live as long as they do now. When someone died at age sixty-five, many people thought he had lived a long life. Today if someone died at age sixty-five, you would think it was a shame that they had to die so young.

Medicare and your health insurance are designed to deliver acute care. You go into the hospital and they cut here, sew there, and send you home. It is not designed to deliver custodial care, the type of care you need when you have an illness in which there is no cure, and you need help taking care of yourself. Some examples of illnesses that require custodial care are Parkinson's, Alzheimer's, strokes, a broken hip, and chronic arthritis. Unfortunately, these types of conditions increase as people live longer.

Let's say we have two families, the Browns and the Greens, both in their seventies and covered by Medicare. Mr. Brown isn't feeling well one day, and his doctor gives him the bad news that he has prostate cancer. He needs surgery, treatment, and a hospital stay. The total cost of his care is $300,000. Luckily, Medicare will pay most of the bill. Mr. Green is also feeling ill. His doctor tells him that he has Alzheimer's disease. Eventually he must enter a nursing home where he lives out the rest of his life. The total cost of his care is also $300,000, but Medicare doesn't pay, he does.

If you ever need long-term care how much will it cost? According to the AARP, the average cost of a nursing home is $150 per day, but this varies widely by state. For example, the average cost in Louisiana is only $99 per day, while the average cost in Alaska is $448 per day. In Connecticut, where I live, the cost is $256 per day. According to a study done by the Society of Actuaries, people over the age of sixty-five have a 48 percent chance of spending some time in a nursing home. Of those, half will spend more than four months and half will spend less than four months. According to the MetLife Mature Market Institute, the average length of stay in a nursing home is 2.4 years. No matter where you live, that can add up.

There are some big risks in life. The risk of your house burning down is 1 in 240 (*March 31, 2000 National Fire Prevention Association*), but you have homeowner's insurance for that. The risk of being in a car accident is 1 in 8 (*2001 National Safety Council*), but you have car insurance for that. An illness could happen at any time, but you have health insurance for that. Your risk of needing long-term care is almost 1 in 2 (*1997 Modification of National Nursing Home Survey, Society of Actuaries*), but most people do not have long-term care insurance.

Why is that? If this is such a great risk, why don't more people have insurance? Insurance companies would argue that people don't understand long-term care insurance and that more education is needed. In my speeches and on my radio show, I hear it is too expensive. I do not think that is the real reason people do not have the insurance. If you have homeowner's insurance, that's too expensive. If you have car insurance, that's too expensive. If you have a Medicare supplement, that's too expensive. When was the last time you wrote a check to an insurance company and thought, "Wow, that's really a great deal!" (And if you did, please let me know what company it was with).

I think the reason why most people don't have long-term care insurance comes down to two things. First, for most retirees, needing long-term care is their greatest fear. Buying long-term care insurance brings the realization that you might need to use it some day. The second reason is that most of what we learn about finance we learn from our parents. If your parents had a home, they had homeowner's insurance. If they had a car, they had car insurance. Your parents probably never had long-term care insurance. In fact, it probably did not even exist when your parents retired. Congratulations, you are the first generation of retirees to live longer and longer. But medical science can't keep you healthy. You are the first generation that has this risk to your assets. My generation will learn from you. We will either see our parents purchase long-term care insurance, or we will see them need long-term care and have none. In my generation, everyone will have long-term care insurance. It will just be accepted as one of the things you have to have when you retire.

I see the difference now in my practice. People in their fifties come into my office ready to sign on the dotted line. Their parents are getting older, and the fifty-year-olds see the issues their parents are dealing with. The sixty-and seventy-year-olds are different. They usually come into my office with a large folder of information they have accumulated throughout the years. They struggle with the decision to buy the insurance, and, if they do purchase it, they do it begrudgingly.

Not everyone needs long-term care insurance. I would suggest that if you have under $200,000 in liquid net worth or cannot afford the insurance premiums, then you might want to arrange your affairs to qualify for Medicaid. Medicare won't pay, but Medicaid will if you are destitute.

Medicaid is a state and federal health insurance program for those with limited resources. If you qualify, Medicaid will pay for long-term care. Please keep in mind that Medicaid rules can vary by state and change often. You can go to Medicaid's website to find out specific information about your state. In Connecticut, a single person would qualify if he or she had around $1,600 in assets or less. Medicaid would allow you to keep only around $56 a month of income. If you are married, Medicaid allows the healthy spouse to keep at least half of all assets. However, this amount cannot be more than $90,660 (even if half of your assets is more than that) or less than $18,132 (even if half of your assets is less than that). Medicaid also allows the healthy spouse to keep all of his or her income and up to $1,515 a month in income from the spouse receiving care.

There is a lot of misconception over what happens to your house if you need Medicaid. If you go into a nursing home and do not expect to return home, your house is counted as an asset. Medicaid will expect you to sell it unless any of these people live in it:

- Your spouse
- A child under 21
- An adult blind or disabled child
- A brother or sister who also partly owns the house and has lived there for at least one year before you went into a nursing home

Now you may just be thinking, why don't you just give everything to your children and then apply for Medicaid? Unfortunately, Medicaid has already thought of this. Under current regulations, if you transferred assets to anyone within five years of applying for Medicaid, you may not be able to get Medicaid to pay for your care for a certain amount of time.

The Medicaid rules are extremely complex and vary by state. I urge you to contact a qualified elder law attorney in your area before you engage in any Medicaid planning. You can search at the National

Association of Elder Law Attorneys at the following Web address: http://www.naela.com/Applications/ConsumerDirectory/index.cfm. (As of this writing this is an active link. Please keep in mind that sometimes websites change.)

If you have a larger level of liquid assets, perhaps $1.5 million or more, you could probably afford to pay the nursing home bill if you needed to. Just like Amy, however, buying long-term care insurance could give you peace of mind.

It's the people in the middle, like Ed and Sue, who have the real problem. They have too much to qualify for Medicaid and too little to pay the bill for the nursing home. For these people, the only option is to buy the insurance or put your head in the sand and hope it never happens to them. Ed and Sue hoped it wouldn't happen to them.

If you decide that you want to buy long-term care insurance, here are a few tips:

1.   If your state has a partnership policy, you should probably opt for that. Currently the only states with this are Connecticut, New York, California, and Indiana, but more are probably coming. A partnership policy gives you long-term care insurance and Medicaid asset protection. Each state's partnership plan is different. In Connecticut every dollar your long-term care policy pays in benefits is one dollar you can protect from the Medicaid rules I mentioned earlier. For example, let's say you are single and need long-term care. Medicaid forces you to spend down your assets to your last $1,600 before you qualify. Let's assume that you have a partnership policy that pays out $200,000 in benefits to pay for your care. Medicaid now would allow you to keep $201,600 ($200,000 that the policy paid plus the $1,600 everyone can keep) and still qualify for Medicaid.

2.   Choose your daily benefit wisely. At the end of the day, the policy you buy will probably depend on your budget. Here is how I would determine your daily benefit. First, start with the average cost of nursing home care in your state. Then subtract any daily income you are getting that you wouldn't need if you got sick. For example, let's say the average daily cost of care for you is $250 per day. You also get $50 per day from a pension and Social Security, and do not have anyone else who would need that income. You should then buy a policy that pays $200 per day.

3. If you can afford it, choose the compound inflation protection. Most policies allow you three choices for inflation protection: none, simple, and compound. In the real world, costs are going up on a compound basis so, if you can afford it, choose the compound inflation protection. For example, let's say you are sixty-five and you purchase a policy that pays $250 per day. Here's what your policy's daily benefit will be by the time you are eighty-four under each option:

    No inflation protection: $250
    Simple inflation protection: $487.50
    Compound inflation protection: $631.74

    Since nursing home costs are rising on a compound basis, the simple inflation protection could leave you short by almost $150 a day. The policy without inflation protection would be short by almost $400 a day. One exception to this rule is that the older you get, the less important inflation protection is. If you are seventy-five or over and decide not to have inflation protection in your policy, I wouldn't argue with you.

4. Check a number of different companies. Prices vary substantially from company to company, so it pays to shop around. In addition, some companies are stricter about health issues than others are. If you are in anything but perfect health, always make sure your agent talks to the company before submitting a policy. It can save you a lot of time and trouble.

5. Don't buy home health-care-only or nursing home-only policies. Many companies will sell you policies that will pay only if you have home health care or will pay only if you go into a nursing home. Even though they are cheaper, I don't recommend going that route. I would hate to see someone pay for twenty years on a home health-care policy only to see him need to go into a nursing home.

6. Assume that your premiums will increase. Many people are not aware of this, but your long-term care premium is not guaranteed. They can't s just raise the premium for Judy Johnson at 1 Maple Lane in New York, but they can raise the premium across the board for all sixty-five-year-old women in New York. This is still a young industry, and insurance companies aren't sure how to price their policies. Many have low premiums to attract business, which cannot be sustained. Do not buy a policy that you can just barely

afford today. If it goes up tomorrow, then you won't be able to afford it. Assume the premium will increase. If it does, you won't be surprised.

7. Apply before you get sick. That may seem obvious, but, in my experience, most people procrastinate until something happens to them and then they decide to buy the insurance. As I said before, most people I meet have a large folder of long-term care information that accumulates throughout the years. Pull it out now and go through it. Ask yourself what would happen if you or your spouse (or both) needed long-term care. Talk to an agent or agents, and, if you are going to buy the policy, just go ahead and do it.

Some people object to buying long-term care insurance because they don't like paying for something they may never need (but don't you do the same with your homeowner's insurance?), or they don't like paying yearly premiums. For these people, there are alternatives to traditional long-term care insurance.

Return of Premium

In a traditional long-term care policy, if you pay premiums for your life and never need care, your family will get nothing back after you die. Some companies offer a return of premium option. Adding this option to your policy returns all of the premiums you paid to your family after you die, assuming you never used any of the benefits.

Asset-Based Long-Term Care

Some companies structure their policies a little bit differently. Instead of paying a yearly premium, you put down a one-time deposit. Here's how it works. If you qualify, you can deposit funds into a special interest bearing account. When you deposit funds into this account, you have three immediate benefits:

1. You receive interest on your deposit and have a money-back guarantee.
2. You receive a much larger amount to use for nursing care if you need it.
3. Finally, if you die, your family receives a death benefit, usually in excess of your original deposit.

This is called asset-based long-term care because your deposit is still an asset. While traditional long-term care is a liability, asset-based long-term care works especially well for people who weren't going to buy traditional long-term care insurance anyway.

Action Plan:

1. Calculate the yearly cost of nursing home care in your state. For example, Stamford, Connecticut, is $300 per day for a semiprivate room. That comes to $109,500 a year. (To keep the calculations simple, we will ignore inflation, assuming that your assets will grow as the cost of care grows. The younger you are, however, the more affect that nursing home inflation could have.)

2. Multiply the yearly cost of care by three. You have no way of knowing how long you might actually need care, so the best we can do is to use three years as an estimate. Please keep in mind that you might need care for a longer or shorter period. Using Stamford, Connecticut, as an example, three years of coverage would cost $328,500.

3. Answer true or false to the questions below:

☐ T ☐ F   I can easily afford the cost of care in my state from my assets and/or income. This can be done without affecting a healthy spouse who may still be living in the home or my children's inheritance.

☐ T ☐ F   My liquid net worth is under $250,000. Furthermore, I cannot afford premiums for long-term care insurance.

☐ T ☐ F   I am single and either have no children or am not concerned with leaving them an inheritance.

If you answered true to any of the above questions, then you may not need long-term care insurance. If you could legally drop your homeowner's insurance, would you do it? My guess is that you wouldn't. Even if you could afford to replace your house, you would rather have the insurance company assume that risk. You are much more likely to need long-term care than you are to have your home burn down. Why should long-term care insurance be any different from your homeowner's insurance?

If you didn't answer true to any of the above questions, you could have a significant problem if you or your spouse ever needed long-term care. Either start pricing long-term care policies or sit down with an elder law attorney to learn about ways you may be able to protect your assets.

CHAPTER 10

WHAT MY WEALTHY GRANDPARENTS TAUGHT ME ABOUT ESTATE PLANNING

My wealthy grandmother lived in a small town. I will never forget her funeral, looking out of the back of our car at the funeral procession. There were cars as far as the eye could see, all coming to my grandmother's funeral. That small town must have been shut down that day, as everyone was either at my grandmother's funeral or stuck in traffic behind the procession.

When my father died we had to go through his personal items. I will never forget going through his ties. He had always been meticulous about his appearance and had gotten great satisfaction from his creative tie collection. Unfortunately, his ties weren't conservative enough for me, and my brother never wore ties. What we didn't end up giving away, we turned into a quilt.

Like most recent college graduates, Peter wasn't quite sure what he wanted to do with his life. He missed college and, quite frankly, was a little bit lazy about getting a job. Then tragedy struck. His father suffered a massive heart attack and died. His father had been a diligent saver all of his life and had left a retirement plan of $1.4 million to be split evenly between Peter and his brother. Now that he was $700,000 richer, finding a job was not all that important to Peter. He could wait on that and afford to live a little. It didn't matter to him that every dollar he took out of the retirement plan was taxable; he had more than enough. Peter's brother looked at it differently. He had a lot of money, but that didn't change the way he lived his life. He got a good job, spent less than what he earned, and saved what he could. Seven years later, Peter had a negative net worth, since he owed the IRS back taxes on withdrawals he had made and didn't have any money left to pay the tax. He hadn't held a steady job and had very little prospects for the future. Peter's brother had managed to parlay his inheritance into a nest egg worth over $1 million. He is confident that his retirement and lifestyle will be secure.

How will you be remembered after you are gone? Perhaps you don't care, or perhaps you haven't thought about it. Maybe, if you are like me, you have thought about it quite a bit. What will your legacy be? To many people, estate planning is all about numbers—how much money or stuff you will leave your family. That is a big part of estate planning, but it is much more than that. It is also how you will leave your assets and the legacy you will leave when you are gone.

Your Objectives

Before you sit down to craft your estate plan, you need to know what your objectives are. At a minimum, you should consider the following issues:

1. How do you want to be remembered?
2. What are the cash or income needs of your survivors?
3. How much cash is needed to pay estate taxes?
4. How can you replace wealth lost to estate taxes?
5. Do you want your beneficiaries to inherit money outright, or would you rather use a trust to protect and manage it?
6. Do you have any charitable intent?

My Wealthy Grandparents

My wealthy grandparents sat down with an experienced estate-planning attorney and devised an effective estate plan early on. They used a number of strategies to ensure that there would be no estate taxes due on their death.

Estate Taxes

As of this writing, estate taxes are up in the air. The table below shows what the current estate tax law is:

Year	Max. Estate Tax Credit	Max. Unified Rate
2006	$2 million	46%
2007	$2 million	45%
2008	$2 million	45%
2009	$3.5 million	45%
2010	Tax Repeal	0%
2011	$1 million	50%

Source: IRS

As you can see, the tax is scheduled to be repealed in 2010 and will come back in 2011. If that makes no sense to you, then you are not alone. Even if there is a permanent repeal, it probably won't last. Here are a couple of reasons why:

1. Dead people don't vote, so it's hard for them to complain about this tax.
2. Even if one administration and Congress repeals it, another one can just bring it back.
3. Most families are not subject to the estate tax.

Also, do not forget the state estate tax. Under the old estate tax rules, states got a significant amount of money from the federal estate tax. Now that this money is drying up, many states have enacted their own rules that you must be aware of.

I do not know what the future holds, but if you have a sizeable estate you should be prepared.

Wills

Do you have a will? If not, you have chosen to leave your assets to your heirs in the most confusing and time-consuming manner possible. If so, you have taken a great first step, but it may not be enough. A well thought out estate plan leaves your belongings to your heirs in the most efficient manner while taking into account their different needs and wants. Your will might cover large items, but what about the small stuff lying around your house? I have heard horror stories about siblings who no longer talk because of fights over trivial items not included in the will. Have you left your home equally to your two children, knowing full well that one will want to live in it while the other will want to sell it? People do things like these all the time, yet it's a recipe for disaster.

A will is just the start of your estate plan. What you are going to leave to your family is easy; how you are going to leave it is the hard part. Do you have children or grandchildren like Peter who should not be trusted with money left to them outright? Do you have family members who are likely to be sued or divorced? If so, you might want to put protections on their inheritances.

Are You Properly Insured?

Will you leave behind enough money for your family to maintain their lifestyle? A simple measure to figure out if you have proper insurance is to cut it in half and drop the zero. For example, if you have $500,000 in life insurance, you divide that number in half ($250,000) and drop the zero ($25,000). This is how much annual income your heirs could expect to receive from the life insurance proceeds. This example ignores a number of variables, but it is a good starting point in figuring out if you have proper insurance.

Bad Estate Division

Many times I find that people have the basic "I love you" will. When one spouse dies, everything goes to the survivor. This is OK if you are not subject to estate taxes but can be a bad move if you are. For 2006, we are all allowed to pass up to $2 million to anyone we want without estate taxes. You can always pass an unlimited amount to your spouse without tax. Because of this, most people structure their estate plan to leave everything to the surviving spouse, wasting their $2 million exemption and pushing the problem off until after their spouse dies. Below is a typical bad estate plan for a couple with $4 million dollars in assets:

Typical Bad Estate Plan

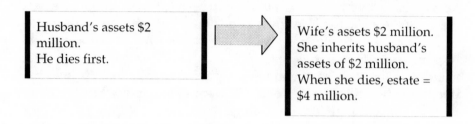

Husband's assets $2 million.
He dies first.

Wife's assets $2 million. She inherits husband's assets of $2 million. When she dies, estate = $4 million.

Problem delayed until wife's death.

Wife's Estate	$4 million
Tax Exempt Amount	$2 million
Taxable Amount	$2 million
Estate Tax	**$780,800**

In this case the estate tax due at the wife's death is $780,800, and the husband's $2 million exemption was wasted. Below is a typical good estate plan:

Typical Good Estate Plan

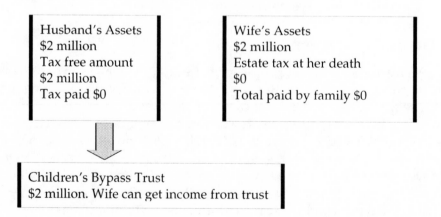

Husband's Assets
$2 million
Tax free amount
$2 million
Tax paid $0

Wife's Assets
$2 million
Estate tax at her death
$0
Total paid by family $0

Children's Bypass Trust
$2 million. Wife can get income from trust

In the typical good estate plan, the husband and wife each own $2 million of assets. When the husband dies, he leaves his $2 million to a trust for the benefit of the children. Yet his wife can get income from the trust while she is alive. Because he has a $2 million estate tax exemption, his gift to the trust is estate tax free. The wife keeps her $2 million and uses her exemption when she dies so that it will pass to the children estate tax free as well. The end result is that the children inherit $4 million without estate taxes by just adding a simple trust.

Lack of Liquidity

Liquidity is extremely important if you are subject to estate taxes, since the IRS will want their money in nine months. In the above bad estate plan example, the family would have owed $780,800 in estate taxes. If the parent's assets are liquid items like stocks or mutual funds, it is relatively easy for the children to sell these and pay the tax. On the other hand, if the assets are illiquid, like real estate or family businesses, it might not be possible to sell these in time or get the market price.

Double-Taxed Assets

Tax-deferred investments like annuities, IRAs, and retirement plans are what we call double-taxed assets. These assets are taxable in your estate, and money taken out of them to pay the estate tax is income taxable. Because of this double tax, your children could lose up to 75 percent of the value of these assets. We will talk more about this issue in the next chapter on IRAs.

Get a Discount on Your Estate Taxes

Here's a simple way to get a 70 percent discount on your estate taxes. As we know, the estate tax on a $4 million estate is $780,800. A simple solution would be to buy a life insurance policy with a death benefit of $780,800 to pay the estate tax. Assuming a healthy couple, both age sixty-five, this policy would require premiums of $22,000 per year for ten years, a total payment of $220,000. When they die, the policy would pay off, and the kids could use the proceeds to pay estate taxes. So, in effect, the parents have paid $220,000 to pay off $780,800 in estate taxes; you won't find that kind of deal at the mall!

Ownership Does Not Equal Control

Imagine the CEO of GE. He does not own the company; shareholders do. Every morning the corporate limo picks him up and drives him to work. He makes the day-to-day decisions on what the company will do. He eats lunch in the corporate dining room. He uses the corporate jet when he needs to get somewhere. He does not own the company, but he controls it. This can be a critical distinction in estate planning. What you own is includable in your estate. Therefore, the simple solution is not to own enough to make your estate taxable. Most people balk at this, however, because they think that if they do not own it they will lose control. Just like the situation with GE, this does not have to be the case. While I don't want to get too technical here, suffice it to say that there are a number of types of trusts that allow you to get money out of your estate and still retain some control. Make sure you talk to your attorney about this issue.

Consider Leaving Money in Trust

Sometimes inheriting sums of money can corrupt your children and grandchildren. I have heard many stories of children who have inherited money only to squander it or use it as an excuse not to work. Most simple wills allow beneficiaries to access assets once they reach a specific age like twenty-one.

Consider an Ethical Will

Growing up, I learned the lessons that most boys learn from their fathers: how to throw and catch a ball, how to tie a tie, and the birds and bees. When he died, I came to the realization that all he left behind were memories and stuff; his lifetime of experiences was gone forever. The mistakes he made and what he learned from them, what he would have done differently, what he did well, his values, his goals, his hopes for future generations, all was lost forever. That wouldn't have been the case if he had drafted an ethical will.

An ethical will is not a legal document. Rather than talking about distributing your financial aspects, you talk about what kind of personal legacy you would like to leave for your children and other important people in your life and what you would want to be remembered for.

Below is a list of questions to consider in designing an ethical will:
- How would you like to be remembered?
- What is your personal story?
- If you could do it all over again, would you make the same choices? Why or why not?
- What are your dreams, goals, successes, and failures?
- What are your hopes and dreams for future generations?

An ethical will could be a paragraph, a bound volume, or a video or audiotape.

Here is a suggestion of how you might organize your ethical will:
1. Opening thoughts
2. Values and beliefs
3. Lessons and reflections about life
4. Hopes for the future
5. Forgiveness
6. Requests
7. Concluding thoughts

While a normal will distributes your legacy of money and personal effects, an ethical will distributes your legacy of values, beliefs, knowledge, and wishes for the future. I urge you to consider adding an ethical will to your estate plan.

What Are You Doing to Make the World a More Beautiful Place?

I recently read a book to my daughter entitled *Miss Rumphius.* It is the story of a young girl who tells her grandfather that when she grows up she wants to travel to far away places and live by the sea. He informs her that there is a third thing she must do: something to make the world more beautiful. When she grows old, she has traveled and lives by the sea, but something is missing. She realizes that she has done nothing to make the world a more beautiful place. So she starts spreading flower seeds all over her town, and in short order flowers bloom everywhere. What are you doing to make the world more beautiful?

Action Plan:

1. How would you like to be remembered?
2. What charities or causes would you like to contribute to (if any)?
3. Are there any special situations in your family—disabled children, people who would not be able to handle money, drug addictions, potential lawsuits, potential divorces, and so forth?
4. Set up a family meeting to discuss specifically who gets what.
5. Find an attorney who can help on the quantitative and qualitative aspects of estate planning.

CHAPTER 11

YOUR IRA: TAX SHELTER OR TAX TRAP?

(Note: When I talk about IRAs in this chapter, I am talking about all types of retirement plans—401(k)s, 403(b)s, 457, tax-sheltered annuities (TSAs), Keough plans, pensions, profit sharing, and so on. Where there are differences in the rules between these plans and IRAs, I will indicate that.)

Chris was visibly distraught. His mother had recently passed away, and he was the sole beneficiary on her IRA of $1 million dollars. The bank told him to roll her IRA over into his own. That seemed like good advice, since he was re-titling all of her other assets into his name as well. Unfortunately, only a spouse can roll over an IRA into their own; anyone else trying to do so would make all of the proceeds taxable income. Chris was now looking at about a $400,000 tax bill from the IRS.

As a retiree, your IRA is probably your largest liquid asset. Unfortunately, there are many people who are willing to tell you how to invest you IRA, but there are not many people who will give you good advice about how to take money out of your IRA in the most tax efficient manner. Think about it, Wall Street makes money by managing assets, not by advising you how best to liquidate them. Add to this the complexity of the laws surrounding IRAs, and it is no wonder that many people make mistakes when it comes to IRA distributions. **(Please note that the IRA rules are constantly changing, and what I write in this chapter could be obsolete by the time you read it. Always consult your financial, tax, or legal advisor before doing anything with your IRA.)**

Here are some rules you should follow to make sure your IRA provides a tax shelter for you and your family and doesn't turn into a tax trap.

Rule 1: Understand Required Minimum Distributions.

Required minimum distributions (RMD) from IRAs apply to two types of people: those who are 70.5 or older and those who one day plan on being 70.5 or older. Your IRA has been growing tax deferred for a number of years, but the IRS eventually wants its cut. Your first RMD is due by April 1 of the year after the year you turn 70.5 (like many areas of the tax law, I think this was designed to be deliberately confusing). For example, if you turn 70 in January of this year, then your first RMD is due by April 1 of next year. Subsequent RMDs are due by December 31 every year. If you wait until April 1 to take your first RMD, you must take your second RMD by December 31 of the same year. This means you will have two taxable distributions in the same year. To avoid this, you may want to take your first RMD before December 31 of the year you turn 70.5.

To do the math, simply take the account balance of all of your IRAs as of December 31 of the previous year and divide it by your life expectancy as shown in the Uniform Lifetime Table produced by the IRS. Here is an example:

- Joe turns 70.5 in 2006.
- The value of his IRAs on December 31, 2005, was $100,000.
- According to the Uniform Lifetime Table, his life expectancy is 27.4 years.
- His RMD due by April 1, 2007, is $100,000/27.4, or $3,649.64.

Here is an example for his next RMD:
- On December 31, 2006, the value of his IRAs was $120,000.
- Before December 31, 2007, he would need to look at the Uniform Lifetime Table again to find his life expectancy for a 71-year-old of 26.5 years.
- His RMD due by December 31, 2007, would be $120,000/26.5, or $4,528.30

You can always take out more than your RMD (more about this later), but you cannot take out less. The penalty for taking out less than you should is 50 percent of the amount you should have taken out. So for example, Joe's first RMD was $3,649.64. If he failed to take it out of his IRA, then the penalty is $1,824.82 ($3,649.64 × 50 percent).

While you can probably calculate your RMD by yourself, I would not recommend it. Please have your financial institution do it for you. The laws are too complex, and the penalties are too steep for you to make a mistake.

Rule 2: Simplify Your Life.

Many people I meet have multiple retirement plans. You might have IRAs at a number of different financial institutions, 401(k)s or 403(b)s from your old employer, and so forth. Under the old tax laws, it used to make sense to keep these things separate. This is no longer the case. All of your retirement plans can be combined into one, and probably should be to make your life simpler. This is especially true when it comes time to take your RMD, as it is much easier to make one calculation and have money coming out of one account than to have several.

Rule 3: Use Your IRA Money Last.

Most retirees I meet must supplement their income by taking withdrawals from their investments. If you are like most people, you have two pots of money: your IRA money and your non-IRA money. People will often look at these two pots of money separately. When they take out money to supplement their income, they often take money out of each pot in order to avoid depleting either one. Besides taking your RMD, you should exhaust your non-IRA money before you touch your IRA money. There are two reasons for this:

1. Your IRA money has some protection from creditors; your non-IRA money doesn't.
2. Your IRA money is growing tax deferred; once you take it out you pay ordinary income tax.

Rule 4: Take Advantage of the Stretch IRA.

Your IRA can provide tax-deferred growth for generations if you and your beneficiaries understand the rules. Here are the basics that you need to know:

1. When you die, your IRA will pass to the primary beneficiary you have named in your IRA new account form. Please make sure to keep this updated as your life changes. *Your IRA will not pass according to your will.* If you fail to name a beneficiary, then your

IRA will have to be taken out within five years or over your life expectancy, all depending on your age when you died.

2.   If your primary beneficiary is your spouse, he or she would be able to do, and in most cases should, roll your IRA over into their own.

3.   If your primary beneficiary is not your spouse, he or she must set up a special type of account called an inherited IRA account. *A non-spouse cannot roll your IRA over into their own.* They will then be required to take RMDs based on *their* life expectancy. This is called the stretch IRA because your IRA can be stretched out over the lives of your children and grandchildren.

Stretch IRA Example:

Assumptions:
- John is seventy and has an IRA worth $100,000.
- Sally is his wife and primary beneficiary. She is sixty-seven.
- Gayle is his daughter and contingent beneficiary. She is forty-two.
- John's IRA will grow at 6 percent, and he is in the 33 percent tax bracket.
- John will die at eighty-two.
- Sally will rollover John's IRA into her own and die three years later.

Stretch IRA Numbers:
- During his life, John will receive $66,360 in distributions from his IRA. When he dies, his IRA will be worth $115,303.
- Sally will receive $19,399 in distributions, and when she dies her IRA will be worth $115,545.
- During Gayle's lifetime she will receive $272,627 of distributions.
- In total, a $100,000 IRA would produce $358,386 of distributions.
- If those distributions were reinvested to earn 6 percent at a tax rate of 33 percent, the total value would grow to $578,359, or almost 5.8 times the value of the original IRA.

Why the Stretch IRA May Be Doomed to Fail

The stretch IRA is a great concept, but in many cases it will fail. Here are the problems that could ruin your stretch IRA:

1. **Your beneficiaries might want to take out the money all at once and pay taxes on it.** If you don't trust your beneficiaries to do the right thing with the money, you may want to consider leaving your IRA to a trust. Be careful if you decide to go this route. Most trusts that work perfectly well for estate planning do not work well with IRAs. Make sure you work with an attorney who is knowledgeable about IRAs and IRA trusts.

2. **Your custodian may force a payout.** This can often be the case with retirement plans left at your old employer. They will let your spouse roll your retirement plan into their own IRA but they will usually make your children take out all of the money at once. To avoid this, make sure that you roll over your company retirement plan into an IRA when you leave your job.

Your IRA custodian may also require a forced payout. If you are unsure, you will need to ask them what their policy is when your children or grandchildren inherit your IRA.

3. **Your beneficiaries might get the wrong advice.** IRAs are one of the most complex areas of the tax law. Because of this, it is not rare for beneficiaries to call the IRA custodian after their parents or grandparent's death and to be given the wrong advice.

Rule 5: Consider an IRA Asset Will.

When you set up an IRA, you are given the option of naming a primary beneficiary(s) and a contingent beneficiary(s) who would inherit the IRA if the primary beneficiary(s) was no longer around. Here is another area where your IRA custodian could mess you up. Let's say for example you had two sons, John and Dave. John had a daughter, Jane, your granddaughter, and Dave had a son, Jack, your grandson. Let's say you set up your IRA as follows:

Primary beneficiaries: John 50%   Dave 50%
Your sons

Contingent beneficiaries: Jane 50%   Jack 50%
Your grandchildren

Now let's assume that John predeceases you. What would you want to happen? Most people would want his share to go to his daughter,

Jane, but that's not what most IRA custodians will do. In most cases, 100 percent of your IRA will go to Dave. When you die, Dave would name his son, Jack, as primary beneficiary, and you will disinherit Jane.

Primary beneficiaries:		Dave 100%
Contingent beneficiaries:	Jane 50%	Jack 50%

Some IRA custodians allow a *per stirpes* beneficiary set up. *Per stirpes* is a Latin word meaning by bloodline. If your IRA custodian allows this, then Jane as John's daughter, would step into his place.

Primary beneficiaries:	Jane 50%	Dave 50%
Contingent beneficiaries:		Jack 100%

The only way to find out if your custodian allows this is to read the small print on the IRA application or to ask. When dealing with your IRA custodian, I would call and ask at least three times: whatever answer you get twice you could go with.

If you don't like the answer you get, you can set up what's called an IRA asset will. An IRA asset will is drawn up by an attorney and is your own beneficiary designation form. You would specify exactly what you would want to happen in any situation. You will need to make sure that your custodian accepts it, and if they do they will most likely make you sign some form of indemnification.

Rule 6: Two Times When a Stretch IRA Is Not a Good Idea.

There are two instances when planning on using a stretch IRA might not be a good idea: when you have a taxable estate and when you own a large amount of your employer's stock in your 401(k) plan.

Taxable Estate

As of this writing, the estate tax is in flux. It is scheduled to be repealed in 2010 and, unless the appeal is ratified, it comes back in 2011. In addition, some states have added their own estate taxes.

If you are subject to estate taxes, then your IRA could turn into a tax trap. Money in your IRA is subject to estate taxes, and any money your kids need to take out to pay this tax is subject to income taxes. Up to 75 percent of your IRA can be eaten up by this double tax.

It is important that if you are subject to estate taxes that there is liquidity outside of your IRA to pay them. This should be done with an insurance trust of the kind described in the chapter on estate taxes.

Company Stock

If you have your own company stock in your 401(k) plan, you may be able to take advantage of a tax break know as net unrealized appreciation (NUA). NUA allows you to remove company stock from your 401(k) plan while paying income tax only on what you purchased the stock for. The difference between the purchase price and what it is worth today would be taxed as a long-term capital gain (15 percent) when you sold it. This only applies to stock of your company, so if you work for GE and have Pitney Bowes stock in your 401(k), this will not work; you need to have GE stock in your plan.

Here's an example:

John has the following in his 401(k) plan:
$200,000 mutual funds
$200,000 company stock ($25,000 cost basis)

Let's say John is in the 28 percent federal income tax bracket and wants to use the company stock asset to buy investment property.

Regular Distribution:
$200,000 × 28% = $56,000 federal income tax

NUA Strategy:
$25,000 × 28% = $7,000 federal income tax

Plus

$175,000 × 15% = $26,250 long-term capital gains

$33,250 total taxes ($22,750 savings)

If we assume that John did not need to sell the stock, he could hold onto it and continue to defer paying capital gains taxes.

NUA Tax Break

Under current tax laws, low income taxpayers are in the 5 percent capital gains tax bracket.

You can gift NUA stock to your children or grandchildren and have them sell it for 5 percent capital gains. In 2008 the capital gains tax rate for low income taxpayers is scheduled to go to 0 percent! If your children or grandchildren can hold the stock until then, they can sell it tax free!

Rule 7: If You Are Charitably Inclined, You May Want to Consider Donating IRA Money.

Let's say you have $100,000 in a taxable account and $100,000 in an IRA. You would like to leave $100,000 to charity and $100,000 to your children. Which pot should you leave to which person? If you children inherit your IRA, they will have to pay taxes; if they inherit your taxable account they will not. Since charities do not pay taxes, they could take your IRA money out without taxes. Therefore, if you have charitable intent, your family might be better off if you use IRA money for that purpose.

Rule 8: Put the Right Investments in Your IRA.

Many people put the wrong investments (from a tax standpoint) in their IRAs. The highest income tax rate is 35 percent while the highest long-term capital gains tax rate is 15 percent. Therefore, investments that are likely to generate 35 percent taxes should be in your IRA while investments that generate 15 percent or 0 percent taxes should be held outside of your IRA.

- Inside IRA: Growth stock mutual funds, short hold stocks, and taxable bonds and bond funds.
- Outside IRA: Index/low turnover mutual funds, long hold stocks, tax free bonds, variable and fixed annuities.

Questions You Should Ask Your IRA Custodian

Here are some important questions you should ask your IRA custodian:

1. Do they accept beneficiary designation forms prepared by an attorney?
2. In the event of your death, can your beneficiaries stretch your IRA as specified in the tax code or do they mandate a shorter payout period?
3. In the event of your death, will the custodian permit a trustee-to-trustee transfer to another financial institution of your beneficiary's choosing?
4. In the event of your death, will the custodian permit your beneficiaries to choose their own beneficiaries on their inherited IRA account?
5. Does the custodian allow beneficiary elections to be made *per stirpes*?

These are very important questions, but I would not expect the first person you ask to know the answers. Expect them to take some time finding someone in the organization who has enough IRA expertise.

Action Plan

1. Get copies of all of your IRA beneficiary forms.
2. Make sure that you have named a living person as a beneficiary.
3. Make sure that your beneficiary designations still match your wishes and that all potential beneficiaries are listed as either primary or contingent.
4. Give a copy of your beneficiary forms to all of your beneficiaries and explain how the stretch IRA works.
5. Ask your IRA custodian the questions above.
6. If you do not trust a beneficiary to inherit the money outright, talk to your attorney or advisor about an IRA trust.
7. Review the investments in and outside of your IRA. Are they tax efficient?

CHAPTER 12

REVERSE MORTGAGES

Sometimes situations call for other options to generate extra money to fund retirement. You may be house rich but cash poor and not willing to downsize. In this case, a reverse mortgage could be right for you.

Reverse Mortgages

Reverse mortgages can be a powerful way for someone who is over sixty-two to supplement their income by using their home equity. The following information on reverse mortgages is courtesy of Stephen Lamoreaux, a reverse mortgage specialist with DML Mortgage in Stamford, CT.

Basics

A reverse mortgage is a loan against the equity in your home that provides you cash advances but requires no mandatory monthly repayments during the life of the loan. If the interest is unpaid, it is allowed to accrue against the value of your home. If you do choose to pay any portion of the interest, it may be deductible against income, as would any mortgage interest.

You must be at least sixty-two, own and live in, as a primary residence, a home (1–4 family residence, condominium, co-op, permanent mobile home, or manufactured home) in order to qualify for a reverse mortgage. There are no income, asset, or credit requirements. It is the easiest loan to qualify for.

The proceeds from a reverse mortgage are tax-free and available as a lump sum; fixed, monthly payments for as long as you live in the property; a line of credit; or a combination of these options. These proceeds can be used for any legal purpose you wish, including the following:

- Daily living expenses

- Home repairs and improvements
- Medical bills and prescription drugs
- Existing debts
- Education, travel
- Long-term care and/or long-term care insurance
- Financial and estate tax plans
- Gifts and trusts
- Life insurance
- Any other needs you may have

The amount of reverse mortgage benefit for which you may qualify will depend on your age at the time you apply for the loan, the reverse mortgage program you choose, the value of your home, current interest rates, and, for some products, where you live. As a general rule, the older you are and the greater your equity, the larger the reverse mortgage benefit will be (up to certain limits, in some cases). The reverse mortgage must refinance any outstanding liens against your property before you can withdraw additional funds.

The loan is not due and payable until the borrower no longer occupies the home as a principal residence (i.e., the borrower sells, moves out permanently, or passes away). At that time, the balance of borrowed funds is due and payable, all additional equity in the property belongs to the owners or their beneficiaries.

There are three reverse mortgage loan products available: the FHA, HECM (Home Equity Conversion Mortgage), Fannie Mae Home Keeper, and the Cash Account programs.

The costs associated with getting a reverse mortgage are similar to those with a conventional mortgage, such as the origination fee, appraisal and inspection fees, title policy, mortgage insurance, and other normal closing costs. With a reverse mortgage, all of these costs will be financed as part of the mortgage prior to your withdrawal of additional funds.

You must participate in an independent credit counseling session with a FHA-approved counselor early in the application process for a reverse mortgage. The counselor's job is to educate you about all of your mortgage options. This counseling session is at no cost to the borrower and can be done in person or, more typically, over the telephone. After completing this counseling, you will receive a counseling certificate in the mail, which must be included as part of the reverse mortgage application.

Common Misconceptions

In spite of recent media coverage regarding the attributes of reverse mortgage programs, there remain many misunderstandings and continued misgivings surrounding these loans. Often seniors will say, "I've heard about reverse mortgages and understand they are to be avoided, but I don't know why."

Allow me to address this issue …

1. The borrower(s) must sign their home over to the bank.

The title to the property does not change. A reverse mortgage is just a lien, the same as a traditional mortgage or home equity line. The borrower retains full disposition rights to their property.

2. The bank will take the home upon death of the borrower(s).

At the time of the borrower(s) death, the property will enter probate. The beneficiaries can either refinance the balance of the reverse mortgage, retaining ownership in the home, or sell the property, whereupon the loan is repaid and the remaining equity belongs to the estate.

3. The borrower(s) can withdraw most or all of the equity out of their home.

The average net allowable loan amount is about $200,000 (for a seventy-five-year-old borrower). The borrower cannot withdraw all of the equity in their home. The older the borrower(s), the larger the loan amount available.

Seniors can receive the proceeds the following ways:

- Lump sum—receive all the funds at closing
- Line of credit—retrievable upon request
- Monthly payments—for as long as they live in their home. (Note: A borrower can receive a life monthly payment, which

could exceed both the initially approved loan amount and the value of the home over a long period of time if the borrower lives far past actuarial expectations.)

4.   Closing costs are high.

For some reverse mortgage programs, the closing costs are significant but still far less than one year of typical appreciation on a $300,000 home. Some programs require a one-time mortgage insurance premium payment that protects the homeowner as well as the lender. There are some private reverse mortgage programs that have little or no up-front closing costs. All closing costs (if any) are withdrawn from the gross reverse mortgage loan amount, so that the borrower(s) need not bring a check to the closing.

5.   Interest rates are high and are charged on the total loan amount.

Interest rates are low—currently ranging from 5.26 percent to 8.99 percent (9/2005). All reverse mortgage programs are adjustable rate loans. All have lifetime interest rate caps. Interest is only charged on the borrowed loan amount—not on the total loan available.

SECTION III

PUTTING IT ALL TOGETHER

CHAPTER 13

DO YOU NEED HELP?

Now that you have the components for designing your financial plan, the next question is should you hire someone to help you or should you do it yourself?

In his landmark book, Values Based Financial Planning, Bill Bachrach identified three different types of investors: do-it-yourselfers, collaborators, and delegators.

Do-it-yourselfers are people who make all of their decisions by themselves. My poor grandparents were do-it-yourselfers. They typically work with discount brokers and enjoy studying the markets and financial products and strategies. To be an effective do-it-yourselfer, you need to be as knowledgeable and competent as a professional, which means that someone else would reasonably hire you to manage their finances. Let's say you walked into my office one day, and I told you that I had no other clients and had never really managed money before. I go on to tell you that I watch CNBC from time to time and read *Money* magazine, so I think I have a pretty firm grasp. Even if I make a mistake, I am sure that I will learn from it and not make it again. Would you hire me? Probably not. If you explained your personal finance qualifications, would anyone else hire you? If not, why should you hire yourself?

Another thing you might want to think about is this. Suppose you are very knowledgeable about investments. You do your homework on a particular mutual fund. You know the manager's track record, the standard deviation compared to like funds, the expense ratio compared to like funds, the alpha, the style, and the Sharpe ratio. Let's assume all of this work takes you three hours, and the fund has a 10 percent return. Now let's assume another investor works with a competent financial professional who does the work for him, and he also gets a 10 percent return. Instead of spending three hours on research, he went out to play golf or played with his children or grandchildren.

Which investor had the better return, the investor who earned 10 per-cent or the investor who earned 10 percent and three hours of time?

That being said, if you enjoy doing the work and are good at what you do, then being a do-it-yourselfer is probably for you. This book has given you the foundation of what you need to know, but there is more work you need to do. For the best source of educating yourself, look for the curriculum required to sit for the CERTIFIED FINANCIAL PLANNER™ exam. This educational requirement usually takes between twelve and eighteen months to complete and consists of five courses requiring the student to master over a hundred integrated financial planning topics. The courses cover the main financial plan-ning areas, including the following:

- Principles of financial planning
- Insurance planning
- Employee benefits planning
- Investment planning
- Income tax planning
- Retirement planning
- Estate planning

Of course this does not count the real-world experience, but at least this would give you the educational base to be able to effectively do it yourself.

A collaborator is someone who makes a lot of their own decisions but looks to a professional for help in certain areas. They might research their own investments and then call their stockbroker to just run it by them. Or they might research what type of life insurance and how much is appropriate for their situation and then call an insurance agent to sell it to them. A collaborator is usually either someone who wants to be a do-it-yourselfer but isn't confident enough yet or some-one who wants to be a delegator but hasn't found anyone they trust to delegate to. A collaborator is usually better off working with a financial products salesperson or finding a financial planner to delegate to.

A delegator is someone who would rather spend their time not wor-rying about their money. My wealthy grandparents were delegators. A delegator needs to work with a financial planner who they can com-fortably delegate all of their financial affairs to. A delegator realizes that there are more important things in life than money; there is finan-cial health, mental health, relational health, spiritual health, and physical health. Of all of these areas, financial health is the only are you can delegate. (While life would be great if someone else could do your workout for you, I guarantee that this won't work). The delegator delegates her financial health so that she can focus on those other areas.

A delegator realizes that there are only 168 hours per week and that the quality of life is directly related to how those 168 hours are spent. You could spend them watching CNBC, reading the *Wall Street Journal* and *Money* magazine, and watching over every aspect of your finances, or you could spend them playing golf, spending time with your family, and traveling. A delegator realizes that financial planning is not about how the hot fund of the month is performing; it's about quality of life.

For every activity in our life, we can do one of four things: do it, delay it, drop it, or delegate it—the four Ds. Our ability to delegate that will directly impact what we can get done during the day and ultimately the quality of our lives.

Delegate It

So many people seem to have a problem with delegation. Either we are control freaks and are afraid to delegate something to somebody else, or we are worried that we cannot afford to delegate work to somebody else. I recently hired a new operations manager for my company and delegated all of the administrative tasks that I didn't enjoy doing and that I didn't need to do to him. Another advisor I talked to thought I was crazy to hire someone to do what I could do myself. He has always done everything himself, yet he is constantly struggling to stay in business while my practice is thriving. In the short-term profitability was down, but in the long run it increased because I was able to concentrate more on the things that are more important and that only I can do.

Drop It

I once heard a story from a successful financial advisor at a large brokerage firm. All of the other advisors in his firm had inboxes on the corner of their desks to receive the reams of reports and memos that were dropped off during the day. Instead of having an inbox, this advisor put his trash can at the corner of his desk. Whenever anyone would drop something on his desk, he would immediately sweep it into the trash unread. That might sound crazy, but this advisor was one of the most successful in his office. While others spent time pouring over documents that weren't important, he spent his time building his business.

How much of what takes up your time on a day-to-day basis could you just drop? How much time would that free up for what is more important?

Do It

In a perfect world, you would only do those tasks you enjoy doing and those tasks that only you can do, everything else would be delegated or dropped. Imagine the quality of your life if the only things in your to-do box were the tasks that you enjoyed doing or that only you could do.

How do you structure your life this way? Use the worksheet below, take an ordinary week, and note every activity you do. Next to the activity indicate whether it is delegable, indicate if it is something that only you can do, then indicate whether it is something you enjoy, and finally indicate whether it is something that can be dropped.

How Do You Spend a Week?

Task	Is it delegable? (Y/N)	Are you the only one who can do it? (Y/N)	Do you enjoy doing it? (Y/N)	Can it be dropped? (Y/N)

Once you have your list, sort out those things that can be dropped and drop them. Sort out those things that do not require you and can be delegated, and find someone to delegate them to. You will be left with a list of worthwhile things.

If you decide that you are a delegator, what should you look for in a financial planner? The key issue is trust. You need to find an advisor who you can delegate your finances to and who you can trust to make smart choices about your money. I am going to tell you two things that go against conventional wisdom. First, the role of a financial advisor is not to educate her clients; it is to get results. Second, your first meeting with a financial advisor should not be about you interviewing him; it should be about him interviewing you.

Financial Education

When you look at the Web site or brochure of just about any financial advisor, you see the word *education* in there somewhere, but what are you really hiring an advisor for? Are you hiring an advisor so you can know everything she knows? Or, are you hiring an advisor to get the benefit of everything he knows? My guess is that you are hiring a financial advisor to get results, not to learn all about standard deviation, alpha, beta, and so on. For example, we do a lot of work on our house, and we have a great contractor. Often, he will stop everything to tell me in great detail exactly what he is doing and why. Sometimes he will even ask my advice on how he should proceed. I am a polite person, and I will listen, but in actuality I don't care. I just want results; I want the closet built. I don't care how he does it as long as he does it. Now don't get me wrong, he doesn't have carte blanche to do whatever he wants to our house. We give him our goals, and it is his job to get results in the least expensive and quickest way possible. If something along the way requires our decision, that's fine. If one of our goals is unrealistic or will cost more than we thought, we want to know about it. But at the end of the day, all we want are results, not an education about carpentry.

Imagine two clients working with the same investment advisor. The advisor explains the investment philosophy to client 1 so that he has a basic understanding of what he is doing and why. For client 2, the advisor goes into much more detail and talks about the correlation of the mutual funds, the Sharpe ratios, the Treynor ratios, the standard deviations, the r squared, the money manager's bios, money-management styles, and the underlying stocks she owns and why. Which client has a better outcome? They are both in the same investments and working with the same advisor; therefore the outcome is the same. If you think that you need to know every little detail of every piece of advice you get from your advisor, you are either a collaborator or you have an advisor who you do not trust.

Service Culture or Accountability Culture?

Near where I live is a grocery store called Stew Leonard's. When you walk in the door, you see a sign that says, "Rule 1: The Customer is Always Right. Rule 2: See Rule Number 1." You can return anything you want to them, no questions asked. This is the service culture and is how most financial advisors run their practices. They care about you and want to see you reach your goals, but to them the client is always right. If they determine that you need a will but you don't want to have one, that's OK. If they determine that you need long-term care insurance but you don't want it, that's OK too. If they determine that you need to save a certain amount of money to reach your goals and you don't want to save that much, that's OK.

I believe that the service culture works great for stores like Stew Leonard's, but it is not what you want from your financial advisor. The most effective relationship you can have with an advisor is that of a coach. A coach cares about you and wants to see you reach your goals, but a coach will take the next step and hold you accountable to do what you need to do. Tiger Woods is a great golfer, but he still has a coach for his swing. If you have ever worked out with a personal trainer, you know how much better a workout can be when someone is holding you accountable to reach the goal. A financial advisor acting as your coach would advise you on the strategy that will help you achieve your goals and would then hold you accountable to take the actions that the goal requires. A coach would rather walk away from the relationship then see their client not do the work required to achieve his goals. The most successful people in the world have coaches, and so should you.

Different Types of Advisors

To make things even more complicated, there are a number of different types of advisors and a number of different ways advisors get compensated. Methods of compensating advisors generally fall into one of four categories: fee-only, fee-based, commission, and hourly.

Fee-Only

Fee-only advisors are solely compensated by fees, either charged as a percentage or assets they manager, a retainer, and/or a financial planning fee. Fee-only advisors do not sell products and will either use no commission insurance products or refer insurance needs to a commission-based insurance advisor. A fee-only advisor could be a good choice for a financial delegator.

Fee-Based

Fee-based advisors will usually be compensated by a mix of fees and commissions. For example, a fee-based advisor may charge a fee to manage assets but might earn commissions on insurance products. A fee-based advisor could be a good choice for a financial delegator.

Commission

Commission-based advisors generally earn commissions on investment and/or insurance products. A commission-based advisor could be a good choice for a do-it-yourselfer or collaborator.

Hourly

Hourly advisors usually give advice on an as-needed basis; they sell no insurance or investment products and don't manage any assets. They charge based on an hourly rate. An hourly advisor could be a good choice for a do-it-yourselfer or a collaborator.

Advisors also work in different locations: brokerage firm advisors, insurance company advisors, and independent advisors.

Brokerage Firm Advisors

Advisors in brokerage firms could either be fee-only, fee-based, or commission-based. How they get compensated is ultimately their choice. When dealing with a brokerage firm, you are usually dealing with a company with a household name, which may give you a comfort level. Brokerage firms tend to have proprietary products and incentives to sell them. They also tend not to have that much sophistication with insurance products.

Insurance Company Advisors

Insurance company advisors could either be fee-based or commission-based. It is unlikely that they will be fee only. When dealing with an insurance company, you are also usually dealing with a household name. Insurance companies also have proprietary products and quotas to sell them. They tend to not be as sophisticated on the investment side.

Independent Advisors

Independent advisors can either be fee-only, fee-based, commission-based, or hourly. When dealing with independent advisors, they are usually not household names. But they have no proprietary products to sell, and therefore there will be less conflicts of interest.

My Firm

I spent a few years in a large brokerage firm and a few years working for large insurance companies. I did not like the focus on proprietary products and sales quotas. I felt that it was difficult to put client needs ahead of the needs of the firm. Because of this, I made the decision to become independent. I had a choice of either joining an independent broker and still being able to earn commissions on investments or becoming a Registered Investment Advisor (RIA) and giving up my ability to earn commissions on investments. I decided on the RIA route and have never looked back. I do maintain my insurance license and ability to earn commissions on insurance because I believe that, if I refer insurance needs to a commission-based advisor who only gets compensated if insurance is sold, there will still be a conflict of interest. Since I am doing the work anyway, then I might as well earn the commission. This makes me fee-based. My practice focuses on the recurring revenue that comes from our fees so that insurance commissions are not a major focus.

Designations

There are hundreds of designations that advisors can have. Some of them have rigorous requirements, while others can be obtained in a couple of hours. This is an area where many regulators are cracking down, so don't judge an advisor solely based on designations.

In my practice I made the decisions to become a CERTIFIED FINANCIAL PLANNER™ Practioner. While I don't believe that this makes me smarter than anyone else, I do believe that there should be one respected designation for the financial planning field like the CPA for accountants. I believe that the CFP® designation will ultimately be that.

Your First Meeting with an Advisor

There are many magazine articles, Web sites, and books that will give you a list of questions to ask prospective advisors. In their view, your first meeting with an advisor should be all about you asking them questions. I disagree. I believe that your first meeting with an advisor should be all about him or her asking you questions. Let's say you wanted to know if I was a good golfer or not. What would be the best way to find out? Would you rather ask me, or would you rather watch me play golf? If you just ask me about my golf game, I could tell you about my great handicap, all the courses I have played, and how great I am; you might even believe me. If you watch me play golf, however, it won't take you very long to find out that I have no idea what I am doing. The same holds true for a financial advisor. You can ask an advisor all of the questions you want, but the only way to truly know if he is competent is to watch him work, and the only way to watch him work is to see how he handles a first meeting with a prospective client.

Often, when I will tell people this, the response is that they just don't know enough about the industry to know if someone is good at what she does or not. I don't believe that's the case. You may not understand the industry, but after meeting with someone for an hour or so you should have a pretty good feeling about whether you feel she is competent or not. For example, one day a few years ago my son, who was two at the time, was having problems with eczema on his legs. We brought him to the medical practice we always go to, and a doctor we had never worked with came into the room. Instantly it was clear that he was the oldest doctor in the practice, so my first thought was that maybe he was the founder and the most experienced partner. Then my son got a little cranky. Now I know nothing about medicine, but I figure pediatricians are used to dealing with cranky kids. This guy started getting cranky himself, like this was the first time he ever saw a cranky child. Now I also have to figure that eczema is a pretty common childhood ailment and that any pediatrician should be able to prescribe something right on the spot, but this doctor had to go out and get a desk reference guide and look up the treatment for eczema. Again, I don't know anything about medicine, but common sense would dictate that there should be a cream that can cure or help it—I later found out that there is a cream to treat eczema—but this doctor prescribed an oral steroid and a second drug to counteract the side effects of the steroid. He also told me that the medicine tasted so bad that I would have to force feed it to my son. I know nothing about medicine, but I came out of this encounter feeling that the doctor was not competent. I did not trust his advice.

Here are some things you should look for when searching for a planner:

- Someone who has been providing advisory services for compensation for at least five years.
- Someone who has a clean regulatory record.
- Someone who has worked often with people similar to you.
- Someone who routinely provides recommendations in the same areas that are of concern to you.
- Someone who takes the time to learn of your needs before offering recommendations to you.
- Someone who considers the tax implications of their strategies before recommending them to you.
- Someone who will review your status in all major areas of personal finance, including investments, insurance, taxes, real estate and mortgages, college and retirement issues, employer-provided benefit plans, and estate planning and offer you recommendations as warranted.

CHAPTER 14

TAKE ACTION!

A few years ago I decided that I should get into better shape, so I went down the street and got a membership at the gym. I planned to go every day, but things didn't quite work out that way. I ended up not going at all. I kept paying my membership every month with the intention of going, but it never came to be. Surprisingly, the whole time I was paying membership fees I did not get into any better shape. I didn't take the time to do the actual work. Just like thinking about exercise won't make you physically fit, just having some financial knowledge won't get you results. The only way you get results is by taking action.

It always used to amaze me that I would have people come to my office, spend an hour with me, pay me four figures to utilize my knowledge and the expertise of my team to create a financial strategy that we thought had the greatest probability of getting them to achieve their goals for the reasons that were important to them, and then they would not implement the plan. What a huge waste! Now we will not create financial plans for people who are not committed to implementing them because we understand there are no results without implementation.

There are two types of people in the world, those who get it and those who don't get it. You can easily tell them apart by their actions. People who get it will do whatever they need to do to achieve their goals. My wealthy grandparents were people who got it. People who don't get it will delay action for as long as possible until they are pushed into a corner and forced to act. Then the action they take will be out of desperation and will usually only be a stopgap. My poor grandparents didn't get it. Unfortunately, there are many more people in the world who don't get it than there are people who do get it. My wealthy grandparents got it; my poor grandparents didn't. Which type of person would you rather be?

This book is not a solution to creating an inspiring financial strategy. It is only the beginning. You now have some knowledge and resources that you didn't have before; what you do with them is up to you. Will you put this book on your bookshelf with all of the other books you have read and forgotten about it? Or will you make the commitment to do whatever it takes to achieve your goals for the reasons that are important to you?

ABOUT MATTHEW TUTTLE

Matthew Tuttle is a CERTIFIED FINANCIAL PLANNER ™ certificant, author and educator. He helps his clients make smart choices about their money so that they can achieve their goals for the reasons that are important to them.

Television Personality

Matthew is a frequent guest on **CNNfn** appearing on the Your Money show and Dolans Unscripted with Ken and Daria Dolan. He is also a frequent guest expert on **Channel 12 News.**

Media

Matthew is frequently quoted in the **Wall Street Journal**, **Forbes**, **Kiplinger's Personal Finance**, **SmartMoney**, **Dow Jones Newswires**, the **Journal of Financial Planning,** and a number of other publications. He has been profiled in the **New York Times**, **Stamford Advocate**, and **Greenwich Time**. He writes for the **Fairfield & Westchester County Business Journal** and the **Stamford Senior Flyer**. He has written articles in over 25 publications nationwide. He has also been interviewed for ESBN Radio.

Radio Show

Matthew was the host of the Money $how with Matthew Tuttle. Heard every Sunday from 10:06am to 10:30am on WSTC/WNLK AM 1350 & 1400.

Renowned Educator

Matthew teaches personal finance to consumers as an adjunct professor at Westport Continuing Education, Norwalk Community Technical College, Stamford Continuing Education, Darien Continuing Education, Greenwich Continuing Education, Katonah Continuing Education and the 92nd Street Y.

He has also taught continuing education to CPAs at Baruch College, the CPA/LAW Forum and through the CPA Report.

He has spoken at accounting and trade association meetings across the country.

Author

Matthew has written two chapters for the Life Insurance Answer Book, the desk reference guide for Life Insurance Agents.

Expert Witness

Matthew is sought after for his testimony as an expert witness in financial planning court cases.

Matthew has an MBA in Finance from Boston University.

Certified Financial Planner Board of Standards, Inc. owns the certification marks CFP®, Certified Financial Planner™ and federally registered CFP (with flame logo) in the U.S., which it awards to individuals who successfully complete CFP Board's initial and ongoing certification requirements.

HOW TUTTLE WEALTH MANAGEMENT, LLC SERVES CLIENTS

We use a method to help you make smart choices about your money so you can achieve your goals and fulfill your values.

If the relationship is handled right, you'll never have to worry about money again! With that said, here's what you can expect:

- Your written Financial Plan will be continually updated, tracking progress toward your goals.
- You will have a written "action plan" with accountability assigned.
- We'll help to take care of all of your insurance (life, long term care, health, liability, homeowners, auto, etc.).
- We'll take care of all of your investments. We will implement a fee only investment strategy approved by you. All client assets are held at SEI or Fidelity Investments.
- We'll help you to design an estate plan and coordinate with your attorney as necessary.
- We'll advise you on any financing (mortgages, autos, RVs, boats, etc.) and refer you to a specialist if/when needed.
- We will coordinate with your accountant to make sure your taxes are as low as possible and there are no surprises come April 15.
- We will design the most tax efficient retirement & succession plan for your business.
- We are always available to provide "coaching" on all your financial decisions.

Contact us today to see if we can help you, there is no charge for an initial consultation:

Tuttle Wealth Management, LLC
1 Stamford Plaza, 263 Tresser Blvd. 9th Floor
Stamford, CT 06901
203-564-1956
1-800-462-1655 toll free and fax
www.MatthewTuttle.com
Matthew@MatthewTuttle.com

978-0-595-40631-9
0-595-40631-9

Printed in the United States
78005LV00010B/297